After recently doing DVDs and writings on dea............ that Diana Davis has written a book of encoura............ tion to the deacons' wives. It has often been said............ break us. If a deacon has a wife with a positive wi............. .... serving alongside him, he will be blessed indeed. You will be blessed by this six-week study on deacons' wives.

> —Johnny Hunt
> Author of *The Deacon I Want to Be*
> Pastor, First Baptist Church, Woodstock, Georgia
> Southern Baptist Convention President

In her newest book for deacon wives, Diana Davis writes in her usual engaging and conversational style to women who are new to this ministry as well as those who've been married to a deacon for several years. Never have I seen so many practical, doable, and effective ideas in one book! I highly recommend the book as a gift to deacon wives by their husbands or their churches.

> —Dr. Betty Hassler
> Editor of *Deacon* Magazine

The deacon wife has long wondered what her role of service should be. This scriptural study with practical helps gives great insight to help her reach her full potential and make a difference in the kingdom of God. Every deacon wife can benefit from this book.

> —Clemmie Edwards
> LifeWay deacon wife instructor in Arkansas

Once again Diana has given us a wonderful tool for ministry based on the truth of the Bible and real-life experience. Written as an insider who experienced church life as a deacon's daughter and a pastor's wife, Diana offers practical insights coupled with challenging personal assessment projects that will stretch and grow participants. When read and studied, this book will be a catalyst that will sharpen the wives' ministry, strengthen friendships between deacon families, and serve the church overall.

> —Jim Bohrer
> Pastor, Hope Community Church
> Brownsburg, Indiana

Deacon Wives is practical and purposeful in igniting a passion for service necessary to strengthen the body of Christ and support the pastoral role of the church, an excellent and impactful tool to touch the heart of your church through cultivating the heart of your deacon's family. Drawing from Diana's childhood experience of growing up on ministry and faithful service throughout her adult years as a pastor's wife, this book is a must read for the deacon wife (husband and older children). We have also been most fortunate to have Dr. and Mrs. Davis lead and equip our deacons, and we are thrilled that others will get this opportunity. With great admiration and sincere conviction, we eagerly endorse *Deacon Wives* by Diana Davis!

> —Chris and Michelle Metcalf
> Pastor, Lihue Baptist Church
> Lihue, Hawaii

Diana's writings depict her love of God and her enthusiasm for sharing her ideas with others. She is as vibrant as are her writings. *Deacon Wives* is full of practical ways to inspire and teach the ladies to serve wherever they go, whether it's in the church or in the community.

> —Vela Adair
> Deacon wife, University Baptist Church
> San Antonio, Texas

It is my honor to endorse *Deacon Wives* by Diana Davis. What a wonderful read, and full of helpful resources! I would love to have had a copy when my husband became a deacon and I had to learn the responsibilities of a deacon wife. Well done.

> —Betty Spence
> Deacon wife, First Baptist Church
> Garland, Texas

If you have ever longed to add meaning and significance to your ministry as a deacon's wife, then *Deacon Wives* is a must read. Diana Davis has once again written a book that is both practical and applicable. She has done so in a style that will engage and entertain you.

> —Dave Rogers, former Director of Learning Development
> South Carolina Baptist Convention

Diana Davis is a gifted communicator with innovative ideas on how to do ministry. Her monthly column in the Indian Baptist is helpful for pastors and laypeople alike. Her recent work with *Deacon Wives* has yielded wonderful dividends. Our church has been beneficiaries of this instruction firsthand from the author during a Deacon and Deacon Wives Retreat.

That weekend set a new course for our ladies that has blessed their pastor, their families, and their church.

—Dr. Mark S. Hearn
Senior Pastor, Northside Baptist Church
Indianapolis, Indiana

This book is a wonderful resource, full of practical ideas to help any deacon's wife fully partner with her husband to make an eternal impact for the kingdom of Christ.

—Heidi Hackney
Deacon wife, Hope Community Church
Brownsburg, Indiana

It doesn't matter if you've been a deacon's wife for thirty years or thirty minutes. You will be challenged by the ideas of Diana Davis and the many Scripture reminders to be the deacon's wife God has called you to be. Diana's "friend to friend" presentation of the "Fresh Ideas to Encourage Your Husband" offers advice that can be implemented now. No need to wait to get started in being the supportive wife every deacon (and pastor) needs. Her ideas are not threatening. Any deacon's wife can begin putting them into practice starting now. But beware; you will find soul-searching, self-assessments that will lead you to search God's Word, pray, and look for ways to serve your church and your God.

—Judy S. Saint
LifeWay Deacon Wife Instructor
Florida

We have needed this book for a long time. It encourages as well as instructs the deacon wife that she has a ministry too. It is a holy call to assist her husband to be the best deacon servant he can be. In many cases the deacon's wife can use this information to say the right thing at the right time to encourage her husband to minister to someone in need. This is a book for the deacon's wife and the deacon to understand the need to step up and take charge of their ministry through the church.

—Roy Lee Saint, Deacon Specialist,
Associate Director
Discipleship and Family Department
Florida Baptist Convention

Diana writes from her heart.
She writes from her previous history.
She is a great godly example of a pastor's wife.
She has been the mentor for younger women and older women.
She has started women's ministries.
She is proud of her pastor husband.
She has led by example.
She has a servant's heart.
She has a love for teaching women the biblical lessons to live by.
She is hospitable.
She is always thinking of ways to make things better.
She encourages her husband and church family.
She has a strong walk with the Lord.
She prays for her family.
The book *Deacon Wives* is the example of the way I saw Diana live her life while she was at our church. She is a true lady of God.

> —Linda Aaron
> Deacon wife, First Baptist Church
> Humble, Texas

Diana Davis has done it again! Here is a book for deacons' wives written with great attention to detail and full of helpful tips. Following the tradition of Diana's other books in laying a solid biblical foundation, this one leads you to a deeper understanding of the role of a deacon's wife. I have yet to find any other resource that thoroughly explains this unique role so well. One of the gems of this book is the diagnostic questions and real-life examples. If you find yourself in the honored position of a deacon's wife, you will find many nuggets of wisdom and even a few admonitions to refresh your commitment to this godly role.

> —Debbie Hammond
> Wife of the president of the North American
> Mission Board
> Atlanta, Georgia

Deacon Wives

Fresh Ideas to Encourage Your Husband and the Church

Diana Davis

B&H
PUBLISHING GROUP
Nashville, Tennessee

ISBN: 978-0-8054-4823-8

Published by B&H Publishing Group,
Nashville, Tennessee

Dewey Decimal Classification: 262.1
Subject Heading: DEACONS' WIVES / SPOUSES
OF CLERGY / WIVES

6 7 8 9 10 11 12   14 13 12 11 10

Deacons, likewise, should be worthy of respect, not hypocritical, not drinking a lot of wine, not greedy for money, holding the mystery of the faith with a clear conscience.

And they must also be tested first; if they prove blameless, then they can serve as deacons.

Wives, too, must be worthy of respect, not slanderers, self-controlled, faithful in everything.

Deacons must be husbands of one wife, managing their children and their own households competently.

For those who have served well as deacons acquire a good standing for themselves, and great boldness in the faith that is in Christ Jesus.

1 Timothy 3:8–13

Contents

Dedicated with love and admiration
to my mom, Wanda Roberts Matheus Riddle,
and to all the amazing deacon wives
I've been honored to serve alongside.

Introduction

I admit it. I grew up as a DK. In church lingo that's short for "deacon's kid." My dad was a deacon at First Baptist Church in White Settlement, Texas, and I began learning at an early age about the amazing ministry opportunities of deacons and deacons' wives. As a child I carefully observed my parents' lives, their attitudes toward God and His church, and their loving ministry within the church body.

Little did I know that I would grow up and marry a pastor. Over the years of ministry with my pastor-husband, my appreciation for deacons and their wives quadrupled. When we planted a new church, our only church members were two deacons and their wives. We later served in a medium-size church with more deacons and a large church with a hundred deacons.

And here is what we discovered: Whether it's a tiny church or a large church, deacons and their wives can make a difference.

This book is written just for you, the deacon's wife. I hope you'll read it as if we're sitting across the table drinking coffee. I'll share stories of how deacon wives have impacted me as their pastor's wife. We'll laugh over some crazy situations that deacon wives have encountered, and we'll shed a tear as we talk about grief, death, and sickness ministries. We'll talk frankly about how to handle difficult people and ways you can encourage your husband and church staff members.

It's a working book. You'll enjoy self-evaluation forms and checklists, and you'll be challenged to evaluate your attitudes and ministries. I'm praying that whether you're a new deacon wife or a long-time deacon wife you'll be revitalized and renewed to enjoy the unique ministries that God has given you.

So here is my small offering of ideas for wives of deacons. Grab that cup of coffee, pull up a chair, and let's talk. I hope you're ready for an exciting journey.

Keep on shining!

Diana Davis
www.keeponshining.com

Portions from this book are excerpts from Diana's articles in *Deacon* magazine. See www.lifeway.com.

Hello, Mrs. Deacon

Deacons, likewise, should be worthy of respect, not hypocritical, not drinking a lot of wine, not greedy for money, holding the mystery of the faith with a clear conscience.

And they must also be tested first; if they prove blameless, then they can serve as deacons.

Wives, too, must be worthy of respect, not slanderers, self-controlled, faithful in everything.

Deacons must be husbands of one wife, managing their children and their own households competently.

For those who have served well as deacons acquire a good standing for themselves, and great boldness in the faith that is in Christ Jesus.

1 Timothy 3:8–13

He's Not Surprised

- Type this Web address into your computer: www.googleearth.com.
- After it downloads, type in the address of the building where you are sitting right now.
- As you visually fly from outer space down to the continent, then state, then city, then exact location, think about how great a God you serve.
- He sees much more than this! He sees right down to your "inward parts" (Ps. 139:13). He sees your heart and your thoughts. He is omniscient.
- What a God we serve! He's not surprised.

No Surprise

You're terrified. Or maybe you're stupefied. Your husband has been asked to serve your church as a deacon. You feel a mixture of excitement and trepidation, and you have a zillion questions. We'll address those later in the study. But for now just relax! *This is no surprise to God.*

Before eternity began, the God of our universe was already aware that you would be reading this book today. He knew that your church would see the qualities in your husband and in you and that he would be selected as a deacon to serve your church.

Let's start at the beginning, when God was creating our world. "Then the LORD God made the rib He had taken from the man into a woman and brought her to the man" (Gen. 2:22). This beautiful picture of a great God, who carefully crafts and forms a beautiful helpmate for Adam, pictures Eve as the grand finale of creation! Can you imagine Adam's response when God brought her to him?

Marriage is like that. The mate that God has given us completes us, complements us, enhances us. Although you and your husband are unique individuals, you are better together because God gave you to one another.

You, dear deacon wife, were remarkably and wonderfully created by the God of our universe. He knit you together in your mother's womb (Ps. 139:13). But even *before that* He set you apart for this ministry with your husband. Read these Scriptures:

> The Lord called me before I was born. He named me while I was in my mother's womb. (Isa. 49:1)

> I chose you before I formed you in the womb; I set you apart before you were born. (Jer. 1:5)

> Your eyes saw me when I was formless; all my days were written in Your book and planned before a single one of them began. (Ps. 139:16)

So this is no surprise to God. He knew all about your limitations, your thoughts, your dreams, your spiritual gifts. He knew whom you would marry and which church you would join. He knew your children before you did. He knew about your accomplishments and your failures, your joys, your sins, your job, your health, and (if possible) your hobbies. He knew your economic situation and physical location. He knew that you would be a deacon's wife. He has a wonderful plan for your entire life, and this is a part of that plan.

He knew all this and much more about you. Today is no surprise in heaven. Now isn't that a comfort?

> "For I know the plans I have for you"—this is the LORD's declaration—"plans for your welfare, not for disaster, to give you a future and a hope." (Jer. 29:11)

The Job Interview

The role of deacon wife is not an official designation. Because you are married to a man selected by your church to serve as a deacon, however, and because marriage is a partnership, your husband's new role will impact your life. Maybe you didn't realize it, but your church considered your own personal qualifications when they selected your husband as a deacon. First Timothy 3:8–13 gives specific guidelines about the qualifications for a deacon. The middle verse discusses qualifications for the wife. Your actions and attitudes will impact his potential for true ministry within the church family.

This book is all about practical ideas for deacon wives. Let's first take a brief look at biblical qualifications for a deacon and for a deacon's wife.

DEACON QUALIFICATIONS

First Timothy 3 describes eight qualifications for a deacon. This chapter looks at his character, his attitudes, and his family relationships. It assesses his view of money and alcohol and gives instructions about how a potential deacon must be tested and proven blameless. Your church has carefully considered these eight qualifications before selecting him as a deacon. How do these expectations impact you, the deacon's wife?

Requirement 1: Worthy of Respect (v. 8)

Your husband is known as a respectable man. In your community, your church, and your family, he is a man of respect. How do I know that? When your church began the initial process of selecting deacons, these verses were used as the guideline for the type of man they would select. How does this affect you? Enormously! In Ephesians 5:33, God's Word instructs every wife "to respect her

6

husband." Think of a woman you know who highly respects her husband. Her view of him impacts your view, doesn't it? Somehow her respect for her husband makes you think even more of her, too.

In informal interviews with forty pastors, I asked their most sincere advice for a deacon wife. Almost every answer involved the word *respect*. A woman, and especially a deacon's wife, must respect her husband. The consistent, sincere act of respecting your husband not only honors him, but it also honors your heavenly Father.

Requirement 2: Not Hypocritical (v. 8)

Your deacon husband is the real deal. This certainly does not mean that he is perfect or sinless, but he is a man with a heart for God. His walk matches his talk. His motivations are pure and transparent. He doesn't playact. His life is dedicated to God without selfish motive.

If a person is serving in order to gain business contacts at church, his motives could be questioned. For example, my dad was an insurance salesman. He had a strict personal policy never to discuss or solicit business at church. I remember many times that someone at church would attempt to discuss business, and he would gently ask them to call at the office. I once took a real estate broker's class, and instructions were given about how to find customers by attending church and distributing business cards. You have probably observed people in church whose motive was to get the solo part for their child or to garner votes for the school board election or to gain power or acclaim. A deacon who is not hypocritical will be a positive influence during business meetings or crisis days. His motives are pure.

Requirement 3: Not Drinking a Lot of Wine (v. 8)

A deacon is a man who is under the control of the Holy Spirit and nothing else. Alcohol is a major issue in our society—a large contributor to loss of life and many health-care issues. Alcoholism creates financial jeopardy and marital problems for millions of households. The Bible says a lot about drunkenness and alcohol use in excess. First Corinthians 6:9–11 says, "Do not be deceived: no sexually immoral people, idolaters, adulterers, male prostitutes, homosexuals, thieves, greedy people, *drunkards*, revilers, or swindlers will inherit God's kingdom. Some of you *were* like this; but you were washed, you were sanctified, you were justified in the name of the Lord Jesus Christ and by the Spirit of our God" (emphasis added).

Verse 10 lists "drunkards" as a sinful characteristic and states that some of those Christians *had been* in that lifestyle, but they weren't any more! The New Testament emphasizes the importance of setting a good example. A deacon must consider his personal testimony more important than personal preferences.

True story: When a deacon and his wife from our church served the wine at a local symphony event, my husband, his pastor, had to spend weeks fielding complaints. The deacon's testimony and influence were adversely affected among several younger Christians who were offended by his action. A deacon must guard his testimony at all costs.

Requirement 4: Not Greedy for Money (v. 8)

A deacon's attitude and use of money honor God. He is faithful in stewardship. He joyfully gives at least a tithe to the church. Faithfulness in stewardship, however, also involves what he does with the other 90 percent! He spends all of his money wisely. He uses money generously as a blessing to others. His view of money and possessions is under God's control. Whether he is rich or poor, he is content with what he has and isn't consumed with money (see Phil. 4:12). He is honest in his business affairs and pays his bills.

James Ennis, associate pastor at Castle Hills Baptist in San Antonio for many years, was famous for this quote: "The problem with many people is they get all they can, can all they get, sit on the lid, and spoil the rest!" Some men use people and love money. Instead, a deacon should use money (in God-honoring ways) and love people. In our materialistic society a deacon who manages his money in a godly manner stands out.

Requirement 5: Holding the Mystery of the Faith with a Clear Conscience (v. 9)

> The basic meaning of mystery (Gk. *Musterion*) in Pauline literature is not something secret but rather something that was once hidden and has now been revealed. Paul spoke of a life lived in congruence with the truth of the gospel where the conscience imbued with the truth of God's Word would have no reason to bring inner condemnation—exactly the opposite of the false teachers' lifestyle.[1]

A deacon is faithful to the gospel and committed to Scripture. He believes in the truth of God's Word.

Requirement 6: The Husband of One Wife (v. 12)

That's you! A deacon is committed to marriage "'til death do us part." He doesn't threaten divorce. He is faithful in marriage, both physically and emotionally. He understands that a good, Christ-centered marriage brings honor to God. This requirement for a deacon pictures a man who is not a womanizer or a flirt. He does not have a roving eye. He is loyal and committed to his marriage. He values the most important relationship besides God—his wife—and protects that relationship at all costs to sanctify their marriage.

Requirement 7: Managing Their Children Competently (v. 12)

Admittedly, the responsibility for child-rearing is a joint one. As a loving, committed partner in parenting, you can help your husband excel at fatherhood. God's Word provides great encouragement for parents to teach their children about godly living and to discipline them well and with love. Neglecting the important task of child-rearing will negatively impact ministry. A deacon must be a family man who seeks to raise his children in the discipline and instruction of the Lord. He tries to set the example of spiritual devotion and leadership in the home.

Requirement 8: Managing Their Own Households Competently (v. 12)

This large feat will not be accomplished without a godly wife. Do you conscientiously live within the income that God provides for your household? Do you allow your husband to be the head of the home? An out-of-control household does not reflect well on your God. A deacon, by necessity, is a good manager.

Verse 10 states that deacons must "be tested first," and "if they prove blameless, then they can serve as deacons." Time will reveal the fruit of a life, either positive or negative. By examining a potential deacon's consistency, faithfulness, beliefs, Christian growth, works, and lifestyle, his character and conduct are proven genuine.

So your church has considered all those major qualifications for a deacon and has honored your husband by placing their confidence in him as a servant-leader for your church. That makes you a deacon wife. Let's take a look, then, at 1 Timothy 3:11.

THE DEACON WIFE JOB INTERVIEW

Please complete the job application form below. The questions are not multiple choice. Simply circle yes or no.

Deacon Wife Job Interview

Circle answers:

Married to a deacon?　　　　Yes　　　　No

I would be described by those who know me as:

Worthy of respect	Yes	No
A malicious talker	Yes	No
Self-controlled	Yes	No
Trustworthy in everything	Yes	No

(from 1 Tim. 3:11)

Your church has paid a high compliment to your husband and you by selecting him to serve your church as a deacon. You may have thought, *My husband's being elected a deacon. This has nothing to do with me!*

Wrong. Do assignment 1.

Assignment 1

Right now, turn to 1 Timothy 3:8–13.

- Read the verses aloud.
- Underline verse 11 as you read it.
- Initial here. ____

Right smack in the middle of discussing qualifications for a deacon in the church, Paul stops and lists a job description for wives. Your church has carefully, prayerfully considered these qualifications and has confidence in both your husband and in you, or you wouldn't be reading this book.

"How dare he!" you say. You're an independent woman, after all. Perhaps you're a professional with a salary twice your husband's. Or perhaps you've been a Christian much longer than your husband. Or maybe you're just nervous about measuring up to God's standards.

Ephesians 5 states that in marriage, "the two will become one" (v. 31). You may have already discovered this phenomenon during sickness, success, or parenthood. You are a married couple, a team. Your husband's ministry as a deacon will either be enhanced or hindered by your character and actions.

If your child plays on a ball team, you're automatically a player's mom. Because you were born, you are your mother's daughter. Because you are married to a fine man who was selected by your church to serve as a deacon, you, my dear sister, are a deacon's wife.

There is no mold that you must squeeze into, however. You are a woman who has been saved by grace and called by a great God to serve Him. God has gifted you with your own unique interests, life experiences, talents, and spiritual gifts. It's all a part of His plan. Thank God for the privilege of serving Him as the wife of a deacon in your church.

This Scripture doesn't tell what a deacon wife should *do*. It doesn't state a dress code. It doesn't say that she must be an A-type personality or a certain shoe size. It doesn't say the number of children she should have. It doesn't tell specific things she should *do*. It tells what she should *be*. The functions of deacons and deacon wives vary greatly from church to church, but the inference is this: If you and your husband *are* the type of servants described by these verses, you will naturally *do* the ministries needed in your church.

God created you with the personality, interests, talents, and qualities needed to serve Him alongside your husband. Any changes you need to make are to grow closer to God and more like Him, not to conform to look like the deacon wives in your church. You are exactly the woman for the job.

You've already got the job, but as you took the scriptural job interview from 1 Timothy 3:11, were you reminded of God's expectations? Yes, there are only four listed requirements of a deacon wife. Will you conscientiously live as a woman of respect, self-control, and trustworthiness, guarding your tongue and your heart as 1 Timothy 3:11 challenges?

This book is all about that verse of Scripture.

The Big Four

First Timothy 3:11 mentions four requirements of wives:

Wives, too, must be . . .

1. worthy of _____,
2. not _____,
3. s _____-_____,
4. f _____ in everything.

The Fishbowl Syndrome

Now get this picture: you're going about your life as usual, and suddenly you notice that a church member is *watching* you. It's called the fishbowl syndrome. And it's OK. Younger and less mature

Christians need role models, and you *are* one. Check out these Scriptures.

> Remember your leaders who have spoken God's word to you. As you carefully observe the outcome of their lives, imitate their faith. (Heb. 13:7)

> Watch the blameless and observe the upright, for the man of peace will have a future. (Ps. 37:37)

> Dear friend, do not imitate what is evil, but what is good. The one who does good is of God. (3 John 11)

> Observe those who live according to the example you have in us. (Phil. 3:17)

Members of your church do not think you or your husband is perfect. They do, however, respect and admire you. They have carefully weighed the biblical job descriptions for a deacon and a deacon wife before electing him as a deacon. As a servant-leader a deacon not only serves, but he sets an example. You and your deacon husband were already living for God and serving in His church before today.

People in your church will watch your reactions to life crises, your ministry within the church, your parenting, and your marriage. They will pay close attention to your attitudes, words, and your body language. And that's OK. Live to please God, and don't change what you're doing as you live in that fishbowl. Just keep on swimming.

Eight Ways a Deacon Wife Can Make a Difference This Week

In each chapter of this book, we'll discuss practical tips for a deacon's wife. We'll discuss dozens of how-to ideas for ministry, ways to enhance your family's and your home's impact for Christ, and the incalculable value of prayer. We'll share effective ways you can encourage your husband, your pastor, and your pastor's wife; and an entire chapter will be devoted to ways to help preserve harmony in your church.

Let's get started. The following tips are some starter steps, eight ways you can make an impact on your church this week.

1. SMILE

This story is true. The names have been changed to protect the innocent. I spent time each week discipling Janet, a new Christian. She had asked about the role of deacons in our church, and she quipped, "Oh, I've figured out how to spot which ones are the deacon wives." Curiously, I took the bait. "How?" "They're the ones with the scowls on their faces!" My heart sank. As I sat there, picturing the deacon wives she had met, I realized that their faces *did* hold a permanent frown! Janet didn't know their kind hearts and loving ways. She merely saw their outward appearance. The next time I was with those deacon wives, I related that sad story and challenged them to smile.

> A joyful heart makes a face cheerful. (Prov. 15:13)

> But the fruit of the Spirit is love, joy, peace, patience, kindness, goodness, faith, gentleness, self-control. Against such things there is no law. (Gal. 5:22–23)

Got joy?

Scripture challenges us to "rejoice always" (1 Thess. 5:16). As a deacon wife, set the pace for joy at your church. Does your countenance convey joy? Do your family and church know that you have joy? Do you do God's work with joy? Do your words reflect joy?

Speak positive words. It was a weekly phenomenon. After Sunday morning worship, I'd stand beside my pastor-husband, and we'd greet worshippers as they departed the service. One person would say, "Pastor, we need to turn that air-conditioning down. It was sweltering in there today." The next person in line would comment, "I nearly froze to death in there!" Many complaints have little to do with eternity. Is it really worth launching a campaign to argue about carpet color or classroom assignments? Don't be the constant complainer.

A constant complainer reflects poorly on her God. She deters friends. She hurts her witness and her integrity. If you've developed a habit of complaining at home or at church, change that habit! John put it succinctly: "Stop complaining among yourselves" (John 6:43).

Christians have something to smile about. The God of our universe has written our names on His hand (see Isa. 49:16). He cares intimately for us. He knows every detail about us, right down to the number of hairs on our head (see Luke 12:7). He's promised us a life more abundant (see John 10:10). Joy is a fruit of the spirit (see Gal. 5:22). So smile.

2. Do Something in Sunday School or Small Group

This one is easy! Because Sunday school (or small group) is the vital discipleship arm of your church, your demonstration of hands-on involvement is strategically important. No, every deacon wife is not necessarily a gifted teacher, but each can assist in some way.

Your responsibility in Sunday school doesn't have to be large, but it does need to be done with enthusiasm. For example, if you're the greeter for the kindergarten class, call every child by name. Learn their parents' names and recognize them in church. Arrive early. Encourage the teachers. Do it with great love for God and His people.

Celebrate the Ordination!

It's the culmination of the deacon selection process. How can you make deacon ordination day memorable?

- Call, mail, or e-mail friends and relatives, inviting them to the ordination service.
- Plan a celebration reception at your home after the ordination ceremony.
- Ask a friend to take photos for a remembrance book.
- Purchase a leather Bible as an ordination gift. Ask pastor, deacons, and friends to write their names and a favorite Scripture on a blank page, underlining that Scripture in the Bible.
- Write and mail a note to your husband to tell him how proud you are of him.

If you're not already involved in the Sunday school ministry, meet with the person in charge and ask how you can help. Use your giftedness and interests to find a joyful place of service, such as teacher, assistant teacher, greeter, outreach leader for a class, nursery worker, class secretary, or fellowship planner.

Your involvement in Sunday school demonstrates its importance in your church. This is important!

> Serve wholeheartedly, as if you were serving the Lord, not men. (Eph. 6:7 NIV)

3. WORSHIP (REALLY)

Do you ever catch yourself going through the motions during worship? Worship is not a spectator sport. Make a conscious effort to worship your heavenly Father during worship services.

Participate in every part of the worship service. Never arrive late or leave early. Sing when it's time to sing, even if you don't have a lovely singing voice. Sing every word of every song as if you meant the words. (You do, don't you?) Make a commitment to God right now that you will never again sing a worship song in a rote, artificial, business-as-usual way.

Standing next to my granddad during worship was a childhood experience I'll never forget. Every note of every song he sang was off-key, and he sang it with gusto and joy. Although it was somewhat amusing to a child, his sincerity of worshipping God was unquestionable. As a girl, I came to love to hear my granddad's discordant praise.

Open your Bible to read the Scripture during the sermon, and pray for God to speak through His Word. Joyfully put your tithe in the offering plate. Teach your children to participate in worship. Kindly assist with small disturbances near you. Listen expectantly and aggressively to every word of the sermon, anticipating a word from God through His preacher. Nod your head in agreement. Take sermon notes. Eagerly anticipate decisions during the invitation time, and assist with counseling if needed. Pray fervently that God will change hearts and touch lives.

Worshipping your God must not be a rote, humdrum task. Make it the highlight of your week!

> I rejoiced with those who said to me, "Let us go to the house of the LORD." (Ps. 122:1)

Worship Him faithfully with all your heart, considering the great things He has done for you. (1 Sam. 12:24)

Come, let us worship and bow down; let us kneel before the LORD our Maker. (Ps. 95:6)

If you're the woman who strolls in late or leaves church a few minutes early during the invitation each week, please take the following steps:

1. Get on your knees and ask God's forgiveness for any person who may have been distracted from knowing Him because of you.
2. Call your pastor and ask his forgiveness for disturbing the most important part of the Sunday worship service and for discouraging your pastor.
3. Never do it again. Someone's eternal destiny could be at stake. And eternity is much more important than your pot roast.

Do a Double Take

Worship is so important that I'd like to ask you to reread this short section, underlining things you intend to do during worship next Sunday. Initial here. _____

4. OPEN ARMS

A deacon wife who warmly greets and welcomes newcomers in a church can make an enormous difference. Never leave a guest sitting alone. Never walk past a guest in the church hallways or foyers without offering assistance. Take the initiative to walk guests to their class or to worship. Many guests at your church do not have a personal relationship with Christ and are seeking Him. Visiting a new church is an intimidating feat even for longtime Christians, so do your best to make every guest feel comfortable.

When you greet a newcomer, don't just shake her hand and go on visiting with your longtime friends. Try to establish a common denominator such as children or interests. Ask if she is new in town. Invite her to attend your Bible class or join you for lunch or meet you for tea this week. Introduce the guest to someone with a common interest such as another preschool mom or someone who lives near her new home. Jot your name and phone number on a card and invite her to call if she has a question. Circle items on the bulletin that she might enjoy attending. Begin a list of new people you meet at church. Keep the list in the back of your Bible to help you remember their names.

One wonderful deacon wife in our church would find a guest near her during worship and set up an appointment to visit with her on outreach night that week. Another deacon and deacon wife in our church proudly claimed the title "back-row Baptists." They sat on the rear pew every Sunday, watched for guests, and caught them before they left so they could introduce them to other church members and be sure they felt welcome. No guest snuck by them!

As new members join your church, your welcoming words and friendship can make a difference. Help new Christians find a Bible class and a mentor. Help new members feel comfortable and find a place of ministry and friends in the church.

Who will include the lonely, the fallen, the wealthy, the undesirable? A deacon's wife can set a godly example by opening her arms to welcome, include, and love every person who ventures into God's house. When others shun or ignore, the deacon wife must warmly and sincerely show God's love to every person.

If your church has a greeting time during worship, use those moments to establish new relationships with members who sit around you. Learn names. Share a smile. Don't get caught in a rut, speaking only to the same people every week. Someone near you needs a kind word. Find her.

Open Arms Rehearsal

Select two of the following, and do them this Sunday.

_____ Find a guest during worship greeting time. Spend more time with her than with old friends.

_____ Sit beside a first-time guest during worship.

_____ Sit by the main exit. Attempt to meet each first-time guest after worship.

_____ Walk a guest to Bible class or worship.

_____ Find a first-time guest in the hallway and make her feel welcome.

---

5. TELL SOMEBODY

Here's a simple observation: If you look at the statistics gathered by many denominations each year (annual church profiles), you'll be astonished to see how many churches have *no* new Christians baptized during an entire year.

Zero. Nada. Zilch.

That means an entire church family has not led one individual to know Jesus and be baptized during 365 days. Scripture tells us that "the harvest is plentiful, but the workers are few" (Matt. 9:37 NIV). Will you take a look outside your church door at the harvest that awaits?

> "'Follow me,' He told them, 'and I will make you fish
> for people!'" (Matt. 4:19)

If you, dear deacon wife, will take this command seriously, your church will never again report a zero in the baptisms column. Nothing revives and enlivens a church more than new birth.

Make your goal to have a reputation as a soul winner. Scripture challenges you to be "faithful in everything" (1 Tim. 3:11). Will you be faithful in sharing your testimony? If you've never told anyone about Christ, get involved if your church offers a witnessing class or does FAITH. Read a book about how to witness. Sit down right now and write a few paragraphs about how you received Jesus as your Savior and the difference He makes in your life. Watch for an opportunity to share your personal testimony with someone who doesn't know Him as Savior.

Do you know anyone who is not a Christian? Begin today to make a list of friends, relatives, and acquaintances who may not know Him. At a recent retreat I asked women to write specific names of every distant relative, hairdresser, neighbor, coworker, and others they knew who might not be a Christian. The *shortest* list held eighty names! A deacon wife in our church made a list like that and began systematically to take each person on her list out for lunch and to share her Christian testimony. God honored her witness.

You have no larger priority in life than to share Jesus. Create opportunities to tell someone about Him. Select a favorite witnessing tract and keep it in your handbag. Carry a small marked

New Testament in your purse. Print personal business cards and look for an opportunity to use them as a witness. Put a Christian book on your bookshelf at work. Look for opportunities to share the plan of salvation at the gym, your bridge club, a community organization, or work. Put a Scripture on your car dash and pray that God will use it to begin a conversation about Him. Teach your children to share Christ. If the deacon wives in your church begin to share God's plan of salvation with lost people, your church will never be the same. Share Jesus today.

I'll Tell Somebody

Will you make a renewed commitment to God to tell others about Him?
Initial here. _____

Always be ready to give a defense to anyone who asks you a reason for the hope that is in you. (1 Pet. 3:15)

There will be more joy in heaven over one sinner who repents than over 99 righteous people who don't need repentance. (Luke 15:7)

Gotta Tell

List ten people you know who may not know Jesus as Savior.

1. _____
2. _____
3. _____
4. _____
5. _____
6. _____
7. _____
8. _____
9. _____
10. _____

6. Mentor a Younger Woman in Your Church

Whatever your age, invest time to disciple at least one younger woman in your church. Read Titus 2:3–5.

> Older women are to be reverent in behavior, not slanderers, not addicted to much wine. They are to teach what is good, so that they may encourage the young women to love their husbands and children, to be sensible, pure, good homemakers, and submissive to their husbands, so that God's message will not be slandered.

Perhaps a new Christian in your church is excited to learn about God. You may mentor a woman who is a newcomer at your church or whose husband is a potential new deacon. The mentoring relationship does not have to be formal, but it should be consistent and long-term.

Make a plan to meet together weekly for a cup of tea and conversation. The time you spend may involve just a few minutes, but faithfully carve out time to help that younger Christian woman each week. Talk about something you read from God's Word this week. Listen to her, influence her, and most of all *encourage* her (v. 4).

Right in the Middle

Take a close look at Titus 2:3–5 where older women are instructed to teach younger Christian women. What's the middle word of those verses? It's the secret to mentoring:

E _ _ _ _ _ _ _ _

As the more mature Christian woman, encourage her to be a loving mother, a faithful wife, a growing follower of Christ. Mentoring involves accountability. Ask, "How has God been working in your life this week?" Pray faithfully for and with her.

If you aren't intentionally mentoring at least one younger woman, ask God to guide you to find one this week.

Make a plan to meet with her. Write her name here:

_____

One of the most important legacies that you leave in your church family will be the impact you have on younger Christian women.

7. GET IN GOD'S WORD

What does God expect of you? What's the answer to a problem? Read His instruction book. He's spelled out His answers precisely in His Word, the Bible. Study it with enthusiasm. Marinate in it. Hide it in your heart. You will be amazed at how a Scripture you read this morning may apply to daily circumstances. If you've hidden it in your heart, it will be available at the appropriate time. For example, your son is considering a job that would require him to work occasionally on Sunday. If you've been in God's Word, you'll have a clear answer for him: Exodus 20:10.

Here's the best advice you'll read in this book: read the entire Bible through completely every year. Do this in addition to other studies or lessons you teach. If you commit thirteen minutes per day, you can easily read the entire Bible this year. (13 minutes = 2 television commercial breaks. You can do that!) There is no better preparation for ministry to God's people than reading His Word.

I'll Do it!

Commit to God that you will read the entire Bible within one year. Buy a book or download a plan and start today. Spend a minimum of thirteen minutes daily.

---

8. THE MINISTRY OF PRESENCE

It's the art of showing up. Your faithful commitment to attendance at your church is more important than you've imagined. The Fourth Commandment states, "Remember the Sabbath."

The Fourth Commandment

"Remember to dedicate the Sabbath day: You are to labor six days and do all your work, but the seventh day is a Sabbath to the LORD your God." (Exod. 20:8–10)

As a follower of Christ, we should anticipate worshipping on the Lord's Day. Make it a priority. Plan everything else around it.

As family activities and events are scheduled around the priority of attending worship, your children will learn the importance of honoring the Sabbath and the joy of worshipping God. There is no discussion on Sunday mornings about whether to go to God's house. If a friend stays overnight on Saturday, he or she should plan to join you for Sunday morning worship. You may find that Saturday evenings need to be protected. If Saturday evening activities end at midnight, your family may have difficulty arising expectantly to worship their God early on Sunday morning.

When I was in elementary school, God blessed our family with a lake cabin about an hour's drive from our home. When my deacon/dad led a family prayer to thank God for this blessing, he vocally committed that our family would never use it as an excuse to miss worship or serving Him. Over the years that lake home was used for family fun, church fellowships, and housing guests. We often spent Saturdays water-skiing and relaxing there, but we always drove into town for Sunday school and Sunday worship. If we went to the lake Sunday afternoon, we were still in our place at youth choir that afternoon. Because the precedent was set from the beginning, we never discussed what we would do. Worship on the Lord's Day had priority.

Let's take a look at Angie. She loves her church and is committed to its ministry. She considers herself a faithful worshipper. If you take a careful look, however, you'll find a few gaps in Angie's faithful attendance. Oh, each absence has a justification, but somehow they've begun to multiply. For example, her office asks her to work on Sunday but only a few times each year. She would never allow her children to choose athletics as a priority over worship, but her son did make the all-star team, and her daughter just joined a traveling team. Her family reunions are, of course, on Sundays. When her family was blessed with a new home this year, they were too tired to worship God on Sunday. Her recent out-of-town guests didn't bring clothes for church, so she missed that Sunday. Mother's Day she spends with her mom and Father's Day with dad. Two weeks of vacation takes three Sundays. Then there's Thanksgiving weekend, Christmas, Memorial Day and July 4 weekend, and a couple of three-day weekends. An emergency day, a sick day, one personal crisis— some legitimate "excused absences," right? At this rate, Angie, our committed deacon wife, attends Sunday morning worship in her church only *half* the time. Is that commitment?

Another aspect of the "presence ministry" of a deacon wife involves showing up when it counts. If your church is growing, you cannot possibly be at every church event. A wise deacon wife makes a priority of attending worship, outreach, and her specific areas of ministry and interest. When the entire church is gathered for any all-church event, she is present. It's a great encouragement if she can participate in women's ministry events. In a smaller church she may need to attend most showers, weddings, and funerals. In a larger church she will, of course, be involved in those that touch her sphere of influence.

The church is negatively impacted when important leaders, such as you, dear deacon wife, are not present for worship or major church events. Of course you are faithful in attendance already, so these words are merely a reminder. Attend faithfully. Be visible. Be engaged, interested, participative. Can your pastor and church count on your faithful, joyful presence?

> And let us not neglect our meeting together, as some people do. (Heb. 10:25 NLT)

> I rejoiced with those who said to me, "Let us go to the house of the LORD." (Ps. 122:1)

> Zeal for Your house has consumed me. (Ps. 69:9)

Feel Inadequate? Don't!

Not that we are adequate in ourselves to consider anything as coming from ourselves, but our adequacy is from God. (2 Cor. 3:5 NASB)

---

1. Dorothy Kelley Patterson and Rhonda Harrington Kelley, *Women's Evangelical Commentary: New Testament* (Nashville: B&H Publishing Group, 2006).

→ 2 ←

The Encourager

Have you ever thought of the apostle Paul as someone who needed encouragement? After his dramatic salvation experience, Paul became a strong Christian leader, a soul winner, a church planter. He traveled the known world during New Testament times, planting churches left and right. He wrote many books of our New Testament. He was a Christian hero! That just doesn't seem like someone who needed encouragement, does it?

Take a look in Acts 28 to see a discouraged Paul. He'd been arrested in Jerusalem, imprisoned, shipwrecked, marooned on an island, bitten by a poisonous snake, and was on his way to face a trial in Rome, not knowing whether he would live or die. Verse 15 tells of some unnamed Christian men who came from Rome to meet Paul and walk the rest of the way with him. It says, "At the sight of these men Paul thanked God and was encouraged" (NIV).

If the apostle Paul needed encouragement, be assured that Christians today need encouragement. We're not talking about applause; this is about the ministry of encouragement.

You might be surprised to discover what a significant impact your words and deeds of encouragement can make.

> Therefore encourage one another and build each other up as you are already doing. (1 Thess. 5:11)

> And let us consider how we may spur one another on toward love and good deeds. (Heb. 10:24 NIV)

Encouragement from a deacon wife can impact younger women in your church. Your encouraging words will help peers, children, family members, community residents. You can encourage newcomers in your church and leaders in your church. In this chapter, however, we'll focus on ways a deacon wife can greatly encourage three specific people:

- your favorite deacon (your husband),
- your pastor, and
- your pastor's wife.

Hold on to your hoodie, friend. This is where your role gets exciting.

Encourage Your Favorite Deacon

This book is chock-full of practical ways you can *help* your husband, but this chapter sets the pace by showing you how to *encourage* him. The encouragement you give your deacon husband can be given by no other person, and his ministry will be greatly enhanced because of it. Your husband has an important, eternity-impacting privilege of service as a deacon.

Please Note

If your favorite deacon is *not* your husband, please go directly to marriage counseling.

Here are some ways you can encourage him.

ALLOW HIM TO SERVE

Don't force your deacon husband to choose between serving God and pleasing you. A deacon will be called to devote a lot of time to his ministry, and it may not always be convenient. I remember many times when my pastor husband called one of his deacons to go with him on a crisis visit or assist with a need in the church, and many of those were weekends or late hours or holidays. When your husband is called upon to minister, how will you react?

When I was a child, my dad, the deacon, was often called to assist elderly widows in the church for crises such as a plumbing problem or leaky roof. Since he considered it improper to go alone, I was often invited to accompany him. My job was to chat with the widow while Dad helped with her problem. Dad would whistle while he worked as if it were a great privilege to serve in this way! But here's the point: even when ministry was inconvenient or costly, my mother joyfully allowed Dad to serve. She was proud of him. *Had she resented his ministry, I wonder if his joy would have been stifled.*

We were newlyweds when my husband, Steve, was a seminary student at Southwestern Baptist Theological Seminary in Fort Worth. His part-time job as a youth minister at Wedgwood Baptist was a great opportunity for ministry, and we were both involved up to our ears! After just a few months, however, I decided that I was not getting the attention I needed. I truly loved those youth and that church, but the growing ministry was demanding an increasing number of hours each week.

I pouted childishly for a while, and then I decided to take action. I began to keep a daily journal of how many hours he and I spent with church work. And that list was a doozy! I intended to show it to Steve at the end of the month and to demand a response. Toward the end of my ammo-gathering month, I sat on the back-porch step reading my Bible. Words in 1 Corinthians 13:5 almost popped off the page: Love "keeps no record of wrongs." I vividly remember shedding tears right there on my "list of wrongs" journal as I prayed for God to give me joy instead of resentment about ministry. Steve never saw my ammunition list, but he did see a radical change in his wife's attitude about his service for God.

It's not your job to tell your husband when to serve God. Be supportive. Joyfully allow him to serve as God directs him.

> She rewards him [her husband] with good, not evil, all the days of her life. (Prov. 31:12)

> Better to live on the corner of a roof than to share a house with a nagging wife. (Prov. 21:9)

BE AVAILABLE

You will find many occasions when you can assist your husband with ministry endeavors. Happily seize the opportunity! Tell your husband that you will accompany him or help him when he needs you. Ask how he would like you to help him. Listen and respond when he asks for your help.

Many deacon wives accompany their husbands on homebound or hospital calls, visits to widows or families, and outreach visits. Others assist with benevolence, organization, note-writing, meal preparation, or bereavement. When you are happily available to serve alongside your deacon husband, he will be encouraged.

TELL HIM

You and I know that you are proud of your husband and his commitment to God. Say the words out loud. Tell your husband that you admire him. Tell him often. Brag about him when others are listening. Pay attention to specific ministries he does well and compliment him on them.

> A word spoken at the right time is like golden apples on
> a silver tray. (Prov. 25:11)

Practice Here

One thing I admire about you, _____ (husband's name), is _____.

BE A FAITHFUL WIFE

They were absolutely adorable. When Steve and I moved to San Antonio to plant a church, we were young and impressionable. No one made more of an impression on us than Wes and Thelma Iley, a deacon and his wife in our new church. They were elderly when we met, and I'll never forget the first time we sat on their back porch, drinking sweet tea from crystal glasses. Thelma chirped, "Lover, would you pass me a napkin?" *Lover!* I could feel my cheeks redden, thinking it was a slip of the tongue. But over the next several years, we often heard them address each other with that pet name—"lover." They held hands in public. They doted on each other. No one doubted that Wes and Thelma were exclusively committed to each other.

Steve's seminary professor once made a passionate statement that a man of God must never have so much as a cup of coffee with a woman besides his wife. I thought that was ridiculous! Over the ensuing decades, however, we watched as many strong Christian men and women fell to immoral choices. Most of those affairs began with something as simple as a cup of coffee.

Flee from Evil (2 Tim. 2:22)

Any woman reading this book could have a sinful extramarital affair tomorrow if she chose. Infidelity does not depend on good looks or personality. It takes a woman of great character and commitment, however, to love her husband exclusively. And it's one of the Ten Commandments, too! Guard your mind and heart, dear deacon wife. Take care with your selection of books, movies, and Internet sites. Dress with Christian modesty. Your close friends should be women. Never flirt with other men or give the impression or opportunity of unfaithfulness in marriage.

Try to Outlove Your Husband!

Love your husband wholly. Try to outlove your husband! As you read 1 Corinthians 7:3–5 for a homework assignment this week, renew your commitment to love him physically, emotionally, and exclusively.

Homework

Read these verses slowly.
1 Corinthians 7:2–6
Song of Songs 7

RESPECT HIM

Let's suppose we asked your best friend, your child, and your closest work associate this question: "Does she respect her husband?"

How would they respond? If it was important enough for God to include it in Scripture, the mandate to respect our husbands must be important.

> To sum up, each one of you is to love his wife as himself,
> and the wife is to respect her husband. (Eph. 5:33)

I know. I know. Lighthearted put-downs are a common, trendy practice among women these days, but even in jest, cutting remarks often demean and hurt the man you love. Jabs and criticism do not equal respect. Make a commitment to God right now that no negative word about your mate will ever leave your lips. Ask God to help you to keep that commitment. Write your initials here to remind you of this commitment to respect your husband. _____

Don't focus on his small faults. (You have a few of those too!) Focus on his strengths. Have you ever been around a woman who corrects every sentence her husband utters? It's easy to slip into disrespectful, demeaning habits that harm your husband's reputation.

Here's a good way to start. *Listen* to your husband. Yes, I know that you can multitask, but give this a try this week. When your husband begins talking, stop what you are doing, make eye contact, and listen intently. Don't think about your to-do list, the kids, or work projects. Give him your full attention. The simple act of listening with undivided attention will convey respect.

Here's a bonus: a man who is respected by his wife will love his wife even more.

Chalkboard

I will respect my husband
I will respect my husband
I will respect my husband
I will respect my husband
I will respect my husband
I will respect my husband

_____

_____

ALLOW HIM TO LEAD

Is your husband the leader in your family? I have taken many informal surveys about deacon wives, interviewing deacon wives, pastors, deacons, and church members. Many comments surfaced about leadership in the family. When a wife appears to boss her husband, his respect as a deacon is marred. Even non-Christians poke fun of a man who can't move until he asks his wife! Marriage is a partnership, and the husband and wife are equally important. Ephesians 5 sets a clear precedence for family leadership.

Would those who know you and your husband say that he is the leader in your family? If not, change that! If you "wear the pants" in your home, it's time to give them back to your husband.

> Wives, be submissive to your husbands, as is fitting in the Lord. (Col. 3:18)

> A capable wife is her husband's crown. (Prov. 12:4)

> Wives, submit to your own husbands as to the Lord, for
> the husband is head of the wife as also Christ is head
> of the church. He is the Savior of the body. Now as the
> church submits to Christ, so wives should submit to
> their husbands in everything. (Eph. 5:22–24)

> So that they may encourage the young women to love
> their husbands and children, to be sensible, pure, good
> homemakers, and submissive to their husbands, so
> that God's message will not be slandered. (Titus 2:4–5;
> see 1 Pet. 3:1, 5)

Ask God to give you the wisdom and grace joyfully to allow your husband to be the spiritual and physical leader of your family. Now, believe me, if you are a discerning Christian woman, your husband may often want your input and wisdom, but the wife of a deacon should allow him to lead.

BE HIS CONFIDANTE

This one is huge. When your husband talks with you about something, does he worry that you might repeat it to your mom, sister, or friend? Can your husband share his heart with you? Can he share his confidences? A husband cannot share much with a blabbermouth wife!

In that same realm be extremely careful about confidentiality in church business matters. A pastor needs to be able confidentially to ask deacons for wisdom and input.

Think about it. Twelve deacons are in a meeting, and the pastor asks their private opinion about a pressing issue at church. The topic is one that should be handled discretely and wisely, and the pastor is prudent to seek counsel from spiritual leaders. Each of those deacons, however, goes home and discusses it with his wife. Those wives are careful not to gossip and share the private information; however, the temptation is great, and each wife discusses it with *just one* best friend or relative. She trusts her friend's discretion and is certain the discussion will go no further. Each of those women tries to be discrete, and she only shares a few juicy details with a couple of dear friends.

We're up to forty-eight people now, and we're just getting started. Question: Can that pastor trust his deacons enough to seek their godly counsel? Can your husband trust you to keep a confidence?

If a matter is private, don't try to squeeze it out of your husband. When he talks with you about church matters, don't inject a personal agenda. If your husband does discuss something privately with you, make a zero-tolerance pact with God that you will never discuss any tidbit with any person. Never.

Now that's integrity.

Can your husband trust you to keep a confidence?

Don't Disqualify Him

When the first church selected deacons, they were instructed to test them first. "If they prove blameless, then they can serve as deacons" (1 Tim. 3:10). Part of that "testing" involved a look at the wife (v. 11). Take the open book test and review that verse one more time. If those words do not describe your life, you are in danger of disqualifying your husband as a deacon.

> I have learned to be content in whatever circumstances
> I am. (Phil. 4:11)

One of the best ways you can encourage your husband is by being the kind of woman described in those verses—a woman of respect, a woman who never slanders, a self-controlled woman, a woman who is faithful in everything. Any man would be proud of a wife with those qualities.

For example, one requirement of a deacon is that he is "not greedy for money" (v. 8). Are you content with the financial resources God has given you, or are you spending frivolously, forcing your husband to negate that requirement in his life?

If you want to give yourself a gentle reminder of God's expectations, put that Scripture from 1 Timothy 3:11 on your makeup mirror. Write it on your personal calendar on the first day of each month for a review. Put a copy of it in your Bible as a bookmark. Tape it by the ironing board or computer. Memorize it. Quote it. Sing it. Live it.

No one's encouraging words mean more to your husband than yours. Honor God by intentionally encouraging your favorite deacon.

Ways I Intend to Encourage My Deacon Husband

- ❏ Allow him to serve.
- ❏ Be available to help.
- ❏ Tell him I'm proud of him.
- ❏ Be a faithful wife.
- ❏ Respect him.
- ❏ Be his confidante.
- ❏ Make our home a haven.
- ❏ Mother our children.
- ❏ Don't disqualify him.

Open Book Test

1 Timothy 3:11 says, "Wives, too, must be

_____ of _____, not _____,

_____-_____, _____ in _____."

Encourage Your Pastor

OK, let's get personal for a minute. Read the two statements below and answer with yes or no. Nothing in between. Just yes or no.

Statement 1. I totally support my pastor and pastor's wife.

❑ Yes   ❑ No

Statement 2. Members of my church know for certain that I totally support my pastor and pastor's wife.

❑ Yes   ❑ No

This is a nonnegotiable. Your pastor must never have any small doubt that you and your deacon husband fully support him. Your pastor needs that foundation and security. It enhances your church's reputation and ministry.

Your support encourages the leader God sent to your church. Read aloud 1 Thessalonians 5:12–13 below, then initial here. _____

"Now we ask you, brothers, to give recognition to those who labor among you and lead you in the Lord and admonish you, and to esteem them very highly in love because of their work" (1 Thess. 5:12–13).

Your pastor has one of the most rewarding and exciting jobs in the world, but it's also filled with long hours, extreme stress, constant interruptions, persistent deadlines, and enormous responsibility. He deals regularly with complaints, death, administrative challenges, unchristian behavior, financial decisions, and crises. No, he is not perfect. (Neither are you!) He needs your encouragement. You and your husband will encourage your pastor in your own unique way, but I've gathered a few starter ideas for you.

SERMON ENCOURAGEMENT

You can encourage your pastor by joyfully, faithfully listening to the sermon. For those few minutes every week, pay rapt attention as he exposits God's Word. Your pastor spends countless hours in preparation. He will be encouraged if you listen. Never make a grocery list or count ceiling tiles. Don't shake your watch or gather your belongings or fidget. And don't even think about leaving early! Nothing is more important on a Sunday morning than what God has to say to you through His servant. Consider beginning a sermon journal to take notes of each week's sermon. Now *that* would encourage a pastor. Occasionally tell the pastor how a sermon impacted your life during the week.

SEND AN ENCOURAGEMENT NOTE

If you, as a deacon wife, sent a note of encouragement to your church's pastor on the first day of each month for a year, you might be surprised at the enormous, encouraging impact it would have. Mention a specific point from his sermon or a compliment about his ministry or leadership. Thank your pastor for serving God in your church.

LOVE HIS FAMILY

Your pastor's wife and children make sacrifices daily. Many live away from their extended families in order to serve in your church. Many have made great sacrifices to allow him to complete his seminary education. Your love and acceptance of his family are critical to his effective ministry. Include them in family events. Befriend his wife. Love his kids.

RANDOM ENCOURAGEMENT

Watch for various ways to encourage your pastor. Write a letter to the editor of the local newspaper, complimenting your church's pastor. Take a photo of his family at a church event and frame it for him. Organize his books or decorate his office. Your enthusiastic assistance with special church events and projects is an enormous encouragement to your pastor.

Interesting Tidbit

In an informal survey I did to ask pastors about deacon wives, a line was left for them to give a generic comment.

Fully one-third of their comments mentioned the role of deacon wives to help teach and model proper modesty.

RESPECT YOUR PASTOR

Esteem his God-given position of shepherd and leader. God has called him to serve as your church's pastor. He has given his life to follow that call. A pastor with a seminary degree has spent at least seven years of undergraduate and graduate education to prepare for ministry. A bivocational pastor often works doubly hard.

When you speak about your pastor or to your pastor, always address him respectfully. Even if you consider him a close friend, it would rarely be respectful to refer to him as "Hey, Joe." Many pastors are addressed as Brother Bohrer, Brother Jim, or Dr. Bohrer. Some may prefer to be addressed simply as "Pastor." Ask your pastor his preference, and demonstrate respect by the way you address him. If a pastor requests that he be addressed on a first-name basis, then of course you will comply. Respectfully.

Teach your children to respect the pastor by the way you talk about him and treat him. One deacon in our church taught his young son to shake hands with his pastor each week. That boy respected his pastor.

Respect your pastor's time. Make an appointment when you need to see him. Don't call his home on his day off unless there is an emergency. Look for ways you can help with his time, such as offering to lock the building or arrive early to start the coffeepot. Don't expect your pastor to mop the floors and do all of the visitation himself. God has not called your pastor to personally perform every ministry in the church. His responsibility is to *equip the saints* "for the work of the ministry" (Eph. 4:12 KJV).

Respect the moments before and after Sunday morning worship. Never approach your pastor with a problem or issue on Sunday morning before church. The pastor is preparing to preach God's Word, and most problems can be deferred to a later time, or a deacon or staff person could take care of it. Similarly, the moments after Sunday worship are critical ones for a pastor's ministry. Some pastors stand at an exit door greeting attenders as they leave. Some host a welcome center for first-time guests. A pastor may socialize informally or counsel those who made decisions. Though each pastor ministers in a different way, the minutes following worship are important.

Let's suppose a guest has come to your church for the first time and the pastor would like to greet him. If Deacon Jones has the pastor trapped to discuss carpet cleaning or if Mrs. Jeter keeps him for ten minutes to discuss the inflammation of her ingrown toenail, he cannot effectively minister to newcomers and other members. OK, I'm exaggerating, but long discussions and complaints should be addressed at a different time.

> Obey your leaders and submit to them, for they keep
> watch over your souls as those who will give an account,
> so that they can do this with joy and not with grief, for
> that would be unprofitable for you. (Heb. 13:17)

Let me tell you about the first full-time church where my husband, Steve, served as pastor. He was in his early twenties and had almost finished seminary when he became their pastor.

The church had six deacons. They were all two or three times Steve's age, but those mature Christian men treated their young pastor with great respect. They allowed him to lead and supported him faithfully. I'm sure Steve probably made some mistakes, but God blessed the church, and its attendance quadrupled in three years. I firmly believe that the respect and support of those deacons and deacon wives made a significant difference.

Stagnant churches often have ineffective deacons and deacon wives. They may be divisive or possessive. They may distrust, disrupt, or discourage. They may manipulate. They may just talk negatively about their pastor or church, or they may simply raise their eyebrows or cause doubt. These deacons or deacon wives often have no idea how much their lack of respect can negatively impact God's ministry in their church.

Respectful deacons and deacon wives can make a good pastor great.

Acknowledge Your Pastor's Anniversary

Have you ever noticed that growing, effective churches most often have long-term pastors? Do everything within your power to help your pastor and his wife plant their lives in your church. Never treat your pastor as a short-term employee.

A pastor's anniversary is often overlooked unless deacons and their wives take the lead. Find out the anniversary date of his service at your church and acknowledge it each year. Make sure an announcement is printed in the church bulletin or newsletter stating the number of years he has served along with words of thanks. Present a boutonniere to the pastor and cut flowers for the pastor's wife, either prior to the worship service or during it.

For five- and ten-year anniversaries (such as fifteenth or fortieth), deacons and their wives may take the lead to arrange a joyful celebration and appreciation event for the pastor. It may be a formal dinner or informal fellowship, an after-worship reception, a picnic in the park, or a Friday evening banquet. Involve many members in planning, and make it extra special and personal. Begin planning now for the next round-number anniversary. Need a few starter ideas?

Research Assignment

Our pastor's anniversary date: _____

His next big anniversary will be on: _____
Celebrating _____ years.

Ideas for celebration: _____
_____

Repeat assignment for other ministry staff.

Pastor Anniversary Celebration Ideas

♥ **Favorite Pastor Banquet.** Plan ahead so every member can attend an all-church banquet. Decorate with the pastor's favorite color, and invite everyone to wear that color. Serve his favorite food. Ask the entire group to quote his favorite Scripture in unison. Feature his favorite music. Invite some of his favorite friends or relatives from out of town, and help pay their way to attend. Present his wife a bouquet of her favorite flowers. Prepare an autograph book of notes from church members with each person signing "your favorite church member" beneath his or her name.

♥ **Thirty Surprises for Thirty Years.** As a bonus gift recruit specific deacons and other active members to prepare and deliver a special gift on one assigned day. The number of surprises can coincide with the number of years served.

♥ **An Anniversary Reception,** whether formal or casual, must be personal and spectacular. This event must look different from an everyday church fellowship. Create a visual display of church accomplishments during his pastorate. Cite positive statistics. Ask each church member to write a note for a memory book, then take a photo of each member with the pastor and his wife at the reception and place it in the book with their letters.

♥ **Themed Celebration.** Consider planning a personalized themed anniversary event. How about a "This Is Your Life" testimony event, a "world's best shepherd" party, or a theme to fit your pastor's favorite Bible verse or favorite sport or saying?

♥ **Pastor Paul Miller Day.** If it's a huge anniversary, such as the twenty-fifth, ask city officials if they could declare an official "Pastor Paul Miller Day" in your town. Many towns will present a certificate or plaque, and the mayor may even show up with a proclamation.

♥ **Anniversary Gift.** If a monetary gift is given, attempt to present a tangible, personal memento as well. Wrap it beautifully and present it dramatically. A piece of art could be draped and unveiled. One church presented their long-term pastor with a new car, complete with a gigantic bow on top. For a twenty-fifth anniversary gift, our church gave our music minister (a tennis fan) a trip to the Wimbledon tournament in England. If you're giving a grandfather clock, engrave a small plaque with a thank-you note and years served. Does your pastor's wife love flowers? Ask every woman to bring one fresh flower. As ladies come through the reception line, they present her a flower, which she adds to a huge bouquet.

The elders who rule well are to be considered worthy of double honor, especially those who work hard at preaching and teaching. (1 Tim. 5:17 NASB)

Anonymous Blessings

A church in Indiana celebrated their pastor's twenty-fifth anniversary in a special way. The deacon chairman mailed a letter to each church member, asking them to do an anonymous blessing for the pastor on one of the twenty-five days before his anniversary celebration. Members submitted a commitment card stating their planned blessing and the date they would accomplish it.

The letter suggested dozens of ideas, and members were creative. Some made a donation to a charity in their pastor's name. Others left his favorite snack at his desk or ordered his wife's favorite flowers delivered. Their unique, personalized thank-you notes were touching, and the pastor was overwhelmed with hundreds of small and large surprises—all anonymous.

Though the twenty-fifth anniversary celebration was fabulous, it was dwarfed by those displays of appreciation by individual church members.

CELEBRATING PASTOR APPRECIATION DAY

Many churches celebrate Pastor Appreciation Day during October, and that emphasis is often led by deacons and deacon wives.

This October

Our church will celebrate Pastor Appreciation Day on October ____.

Ideas: _____

_____

_____

This special day encourages the pastor, unites church members, and demonstrates to guests that you have a loving church and a loved leader. If your church has multiple staff, don't forget the associate pastors. Pastor Appreciation Day doesn't have to involve expensive gifts, but early planning is required. According to Scripture, your pastor is worthy of double honor.

Pastor Appreciation Day Ideas

The following starter ideas are excerpts from my book *Fresh Ideas—1,000 Ways to Grow a Thriving and Energetic Church* (B&H Publishing, 2007). Select one of these or concoct your own method of demonstrating appreciation to your church's pastor.

♥ **Here's Your Sign.** Present him a "Best Pastor in Madison" T-shirt, substituting your town's name.

♥ **Stuffed Mailbox.** Distribute stamped envelopes to each church member, pre-addressed to your pastor. Ask them to send a specific, personal note of appreciation this week.

♥ **Church Photo.** Present your pastor with a beautifully framed photo or painting of the church building. Use an extra-wide mat and ask all church members to sign the mat before adding glass.

♥ **A Jillion M&Ms.** Consider one small thing your pastor enjoys—fishing lures, popcorn, coffee, etc. Ask each member, including youth and children, to bring the item on Sunday, for example one bag, any size, of M&Ms. As you thank God for your pastor on Sunday, all members can come to the front and place their token of love in a large basket. Bring extras for guests and those who forget.

♥ **E-pounding.** Distribute your pastor's office e-mail address and a note of instruction to all church attenders, inviting them to write an e-mail of thanks and encouragement to the pastor. Everyone should send the e-mail on a specific day or week, creating an e-pounding of blessings.

♥ **Puzzle Gift.** Take a digital photo of the church building or a group photo of Sunday morning worshippers outside the church building. A puzzle company (for example, puzzles.com) can create a one hundred- or one thousand-piece jigsaw puzzle, printing the church name across the bottom. If you desire, they can add word balloons above a few heads, such as "We love Pastor Jim!"

♥ **Extra! Extra!** This takes planning, but what a splash! Take out a full-page ad in your local newspaper featuring a photo of your pastor with each church member's signature on a border around it. Include a declaration of your church's love and appreciation for the pastor.

♥ **Individual Commentaries.** Purchase a full set of Bible commentaries, presenting one or more books of the set from each Sunday school class, with class members' signatures on the front page.

♥ **Deacon Idea.** Each deacon purchases a gift certificate to a restaurant, car wash, coffee shop, etc. and writes a personal note on it. Present a card with all the coupons.

♥ **While You Were Out.** Do a surprise office makeover (with the pastor's wife's input, of course). Hanover Baptist Church in Indiana surprised their pastor with a fabulous new home office, converted from an unused bedroom. While he was out of town for a few days, new paint, draperies, shelves, desk, chair, computer, and decorator items were added.

♥ **The Gift of Prayer.** You already pray for your pastor, but this visual commitment could affirm that fact to him. Create a form to collect prayer commitments from church members. Ask every church member to choose a specific day of the week and time of day, and commit to pray for their pastor weekly at that time. For example, Ann may elect to pray at seven a.m. each Monday while she drives to work. Several may have the same prayer time, but that is not a problem. Collect the commitment forms, and create a chart for the pastor to see who is praying for him each day. This may be your pastor's favorite gift ever!

♥ **Kids Love Their Pastor.** Why not invite children to draw on a bookmark for their pastor? Youth could paper the pastor's lawn with giant love notes and hearts and balloons (but no toilet paper, please).

♥ **More Ideas.** A trip. A book. A suit for the pastor, a dress for his wife. Theater or sports tickets. Flowers delivered to his wife. Babysitting coupons. A new car (I had to throw that one in!). Restaurant certificates. Cowboy boots. Magazine subscriptions. Tires. Computer software. A tree. You could even "borrow" his car, have it detailed, oiled and lubed, and fill it with gas.

♥ **Stretch It Out.** Want to make Pastor Appreciation Day last even longer? Ask each deacon and deacon wife to choose one day on the October calendar to demonstrate personal appreciation to the pastor. Leave the details totally to each couple. Each one plans a unique way to express appreciation on their assigned day—a note, a gift, a shoeshine, a thank-you balloon bouquet, a meal, etc. Won't your pastor feel appreciated? And won't God be honored by your acts of love for His servant?

Encourage Your Pastor's Wife

For the first thirty years of our marriage, my husband was a pastor. He now serves as the executive director for the State Convention of Baptists in Indiana, so we worship in different churches across our state every week and sometimes several times in a week. I've observed pastors' wives in large and small churches, rural and urban churches, joyful and fighting churches, growing and dormant churches. I believe I've learned more about pastors' wives in these past four years than in thirty years of being one!

Dear deacon wife, you probably don't realize the importance of your encouragement to your pastor's wife and other ministry staff members' wives. Each pastor's or minister's wife endures unique pressures and expectations and responsibilities. Mix those with her family, her profession, her personality and gifts, and your unique church. Some people in your church have unrealistic expectations of her. She walks hand in hand with a pastor who spends many hours a week studying for sermons, dealing with administrative challenges, ministering to church members and strangers in crisis, death, divorce, and depression. He is on call 24-7. Additionally, pastoral families often serve far from their extended families.

Your consistent, caring, positive words of encouragement and acceptance can help give her joy when her ministry burden feels heavy.

May I suggest fourteen phrases to help you encourage your pastor's wife? Few of these will cost you money. Most are simple to accomplish. Many are mere words and attitudes. Use these phrases often. Use them prayerfully.

"It's a Rule . . ."

Make a rule at your church pitch-ins or potluck dinners that the pastor's wife is exempt from bringing a dish. Better yet, call to tell her you're preparing a dish for her, so she needn't cook. When inviting the pastor and his wife to a Sunday school class fellowship or deacon picnic, a written invitation should state, "You're our guest. Don't bring a thing but yourself!"

It sounds trivial, but, believe me, it will make a difference. You may attend a few church events, but the pastor and his wife are often invited to multiple events weekly. I recall one day as a pastor's wife when I had to prepare three separate potluck dishes plus dinner for our children and the babysitter before we could leave to attend church Christmas parties. Even if she loves to cook, food preparations can become costly and burdensome. Exempt her!

"What Do You Think?"

Ask your pastor's wife's opinion. Respect her answers. Learn from your pastor's wife as you minister alongside her.

"I Will Never . . ."

If you haven't said these words to your pastor's wife, say them this week. A deacon's wife once assured me, "If you ever hear that I said something negative about you or the pastor, you will know that it isn't true. I will never say a negative word about my pastor or pastor's family."

Essentially, you're saying, "We're on the same side!" It is vital to church health for a deacon's wife to speak well of her pastor and pastor's wife. If a deacon's wife is scripturally mandated never to be a malicious talker (v. 11), then that directive applies doubly to her conversation about her pastor and pastor's wife! Make a recommitment to God right now to speak positively about His servants. Initial here. _____

"No Problem."

Give her space. Invite her; don't *expect* her. Never be demanding of your pastor's wife's time or attention. Be understanding, tolerant, and loving.

"Let's Do Lunch."

Because you are a woman who is worthy of respect, self-controlled, faithful, and not a gossip (v. 11), your pastor's wife may value a chance to spend individual time with you. No, she cannot be a best friend with every deacon wife, but your offer of friendship and encouragement demonstrates valuable support. Schedule ahead to take her for lunch, your treat! Or invite her to your home for tea, or take her to your favorite dessert shop. Listen more than you talk, and don't have a hidden agenda. Ask God to give you words to encourage her. Listen carefully to discover ways you can pray for your pastor's wife and areas where you can assist her in ministry. Even better, arrange for all the deacon wives to meet her for lunch on her birthday.

A deacon's wife in our church took me (her pastor's wife) out for a birthday lunch annually. I looked forward to it and felt pampered. Another deacon's wife would call occasionally to invite me to meet her at a coffee shop. Even if I couldn't join her, I would feel encouraged because she called.

"Our Former Pastor's Wife . . ."

Stop talking about your former pastor's wife. As I listen to pastors' wives, they often comment about overcomparisons with their predecessors, even decades after they served in a church. For example, one brand-new pastor's wife was surprised when the women's retreat speaker was the former pastor's wife. The event could have been a great launching point to welcome her and for women in the church to get to know her. Instead, she was not acknowledged or even introduced as the new pastor's wife! Of course you are not intentionally hurtful, but it may be best to stop the comparisons.

"HERE'S YOUR FAVORITE _____."

How well do you know your pastor's wife? If you care enough to know something about her, you can minister more effectively with her. It's a little like knowing her love language. Pay attention to her interests, collections, and passions. Know her birth date, her favorite color, her favorite decor. Little things mean a lot when they're personalized.

"HOW CAN I HELP?"

Many pastor wives have more responsibilities than they can humanly accomplish. Carefully observe to discover ways you can assist her. Does she have another set of overnight guests arriving? Let her know you're bringing your world-famous casserole. Offer to help prepare, decorate, serve, or clean. Ask her for a specific way you can help, or offer a suggestion. Instead of "Call me," say, "I'm free from two to four that afternoon. What can I do to help you?"

I was in a growing church last month and observed a deacon's wife in action. She had developed a relationship with the pastor's preschool children, and she joyfully sat with them at the fellowship luncheon, allowing the pastor's wife to socialize with church members. What a help!

During the years I was a pastor's wife, I was able to enjoy many projects, hospitality events, and ministries that could never have been accomplished without the help of deacon wives in our church.

"I Appreciate . . ."

An occasional word of appreciation can revive an exhausted or discouraged pastor's wife. Send notes of encouragement. Give specific examples and sincere compliments. No, she is not serving God for man's appreciation, but Paul admonished us to "encourage one another." Say the words, "Thank you." You would probably be surprised how rarely she hears them.

For several years an anonymous deacon wife in our church mailed encouragement notes addressed to me, her pastor's wife. Some included a Scripture or bookmark. One day I came home to find a wrapped gift on my porch. Each note included this signature, "From a deacon's wife who prays for you." They were sent randomly, unexpectedly, but every note was timed perfectly by God. To this day I don't know which deacon wife sent those encouragements to me. (And, believe me, I was really nice to every one of them, always wondering if she might be my "secret encourager.")

"Will You Join Us?"

Be a friend to your pastor's wife and her family. If they have no plans for a holiday, invite them to join you. If you are blessed with a lake cottage, offer to lend it to your pastor's family for a vacation day. Invite them to join you for Sunday lunch, your treat.

"You Can Count on Me."

Practice this answer: "Certainly!" If your pastor's wife asks for your help, do your best to say yes and to help more than asked. If she suggests a ministry idea for the church, be the first to sign up or volunteer. A deacon wife's encouragement is important to her.

When one pastor's wife led out to begin a women's ministry at her church, many women became involved in Bible classes, missions, and ministry teams. Her only disappointment was the lack of participation by deacon wives! Though they jumped on board later, their early, enthusiastic support would have encouraged that pastor's wife and other women in the church.

When I was a pastor's wife, I once asked our deacon chairman's wife if she thought our deacon wives would consider helping me by serving snacks at the monthly new members' reception at our home. I couldn't believe her answer! She quickly and joyfully arranged a rotating schedule of deacon wives who wanted to help. They not only served; they took over! They brought fabulous snacks on pretty glass trays and fresh flowers or seasonal centerpieces every month. They served graciously, spit-shined my kitchen quietly, and loved doing it! All I had to do was plug in the coffeepot. Their enthusiastic help changed a difficult monthly task into a delight at our home. Say yes.

"Please Call Me If . . ."

One of the most comforting things a deacon and his wife ever said to me was, "If you ever have a flat tire or car trouble and can't reach Pastor Steve, please call us. Put our number in your cell phone." I was a pastor's wife in a new city with three small children, living hundreds of miles from relatives. What a gift!

Tell your pastor's wife specific ways you would enjoy helping her. Would you be available to accompany her if she has a hospital or homebound visit to make? Would you like her to let you know when a member is ill and needs a meal delivered?

A deacon wife once told me that she would be glad to minister to any woman who has a stillborn child. I thought it was touching that she would use her life experience to help others. Little did I know that I would call on her three times during the coming years to comfort women in that exact crisis.

Another deacon wife once said, "If you ever know of a church member with a monetary need, whether it's $10 or $100, will you please give me the privilege of helping anonymously?" A pastor's wife is aware of many needs, and that simple offer from a deacon wife helped a teen attend camp, aided a young mother with diapers, and several others during those next years.

"I LIKE YOU."

Well, you may not say it just like that, but your pastor's wife should know that you like her. A new pastor's wife should not have to earn your friendship or respect. Show respect for her because of her position. Make a point to introduce her to your friends. Honor her by inviting her to give the welcome greeting at women's events or introducing her respectfully. Invite her to greet at the door for your annual women's retreat. Many of our African-American churches address their pastor's wife as First Lady, and some even hire or enlist an assistant to help her.

Encourage the pastor's children. Learn their names. Know something about them. Compliment them. Encourage them. Don't allow others to hold the pastor's children to a different standard than other children. If you see a group of children misbehaving, never call out the pastor's child from among them. If you enjoy children, offer to babysit the pastor's children during weddings and funerals or to be a substitute grandma.

When our daughter was the school mascot, a deacon's wife volunteered to sew accessories and props for her giant owl costume. Autumn and that deacon wife became fast friends. As we were leaving for vacation one year, a deacon and his wife pulled into our driveway. They gave us two $100 bills with instructions to do something fun with our three teenagers. We got to go river-rafting because of that gift! If you have the opportunity, bless your pastor's children in some way.

"I Pray for You."

Four powerful words. Say them often. And do it.

Word Search

Find 21 ways to encourage your pastor's wife.*

E	L	I	M	S	E	T	O	N	T	A
N	T	P	E	C	C	A	R	E	I	M
C	E	A	Y	A	R	P	C	T	T	E
O	S	L	I	S	L	U	N	C	H	N
U	I	E	I	C	D	S	E	E	E	W
R	A	S	K	O	E	P	A	T	N	O
A	R	I	R	V	S	R	S	O	J	L
G	P	T	O	E	P	I	P	R	O	L
E	N	L	R	P	L	E	H	P	Y	O
I	N	V	I	T	E	H	T	I	A	F

*words listed at the end of the chapter

I am amazed at the wide variety of women who are pastors' wives. Some pastors' wives have no children, and others have six children. Some have little education; others earned seminary or doctoral degrees. Some are involved in many areas of the church ministry, and others simply attend faithfully. Some don't mind the spotlight; others prefer to stay behind the scenes.

Vocationally the range is vast. Look at this list of professions of a few pastors' wives I know: nurse, factory worker, college professor, homemaker, salesperson, author, attorney, candle maker, doctor, barrel racer, counselor, hospital chaplain, secretary, school principal, stay-at-home mom, radio announcer, principal, bakery worker, city manager, photographer.

Contrary to popular belief, not every pastor's wife is gifted to play the piano and teach the ladies Sunday school class. Here are a few unique church ministries of some of our Indiana pastors' wives:

Drummer
Church chef
Greeter
Janitor
Web master
Decorator
Landscaper
Music leader
Drama team
Marimbist
Parade float designer
Baptistery assistant
Women's ministry leader
Newsletter editor
Prayer ministry

Here's the point, dear deacon wife: There is no cookie-cutter pastor's wife. Your pastor's wife *is* the perfect, God-given pastor's wife for your church. She is a unique, God-created individual who is married to your pastor. She answers to God, not to you. Be careful never to intimidate or critique her. Allow her total freedom to serve God however she desires within your church.

Encourage your pastor's wife.

Assignment

Say one of these phrases to your pastor's wife this week:
- ❑ It's a rule . . .
- ❑ What do you think?
- ❑ I will never . . .
- ❑ No problem.
- ❑ Let's do lunch.
- ❑ ~~Our former pastor's wife . . .~~
- ❑ Here's your favorite . . .
- ❑ How can I help?
- ❑ I appreciate . . .
- ❑ Will you join us for . . . ?
- ❑ You can count on me.
- ❑ Please call me if . . .
- ❑ I like you.
- ❑ I pray for you.

Do You Know Your Pastor and Church Staff Wives? List names below. Make additional copies if needed.	I'd recognize her anywhere.	I know her children's names.	I've invited her to my home.	I pray for her faithfully.	I've assisted her with a ministry.	She knows she can call me for help.	I've sent notes to encourage her.	I know her well enough to know specific ministry needs.	I know her well enough to know specific personal needs.

*Answers for Word Search: appreciate, ask, enjoy, smile, follow, praise, help, introduce, invite, protect, care, lunch, notes, accept, listen, pray, love, hear, faith, sit, respect.

As for Me and My House

I will lead a life of integrity in my own home.

—PSALM 101:2 NLT

Two of your favorite topics are ahead: your family and your home. Two of your favorite Scriptures, Joshua 24:15 and Hebrews 13:2, will set the pace for this chapter.

Pop Test

"Wives, too, must be worthy of r_____,
not s_____, s_____-c_____ed,
f_____ful in everything" (1 Tim. 3:11).

> ## Consider This
>
> For most women the years of child-rearing will consume only about *one-third of their adult years*. Make every moment count!

The Deacon's Family

Suddenly the deacon's family takes on a new importance. Did you notice this phrase in the 1 Timothy 3 lists of qualifications for a deacon: "*managing their children and their own households competently*"? Scripture clearly teaches parents about training, disciplining, and teaching children. Though every Christian parent is responsible to God to train up their children, a specific reminder is given for the deacon. As you and your husband do your best to manage your children and household competently, others in the church are observing. When you model Christian parenting and living, God is uplifted.

IT'S SHORTER THAN YOU THINK

The years of teaching your children are brief and strategic. Consider this: for the average woman the years of child-rearing will consume only one-third of her adult years. Make the most of those years. Enjoy them. Work hard at rearing godly children. It's worth the effort.

> As for me and my family, we will worship the LORD. (Josh. 24:15)

SET APART

Your family should look different from the lost world. When I was a girl, my parents often reminded me, "Don't forget whose you are!" They weren't referring to the fact that I was a Matheus; they were reminding me that, even as a kid, I was representing my heavenly Father!

Teach your children to love God's church. Help them discover their spiritual gifts and use them. Teach them the joy of tithing. Create traditions. Set parameters for proper priorities. Help them discover biblical answers to their problems. Teach them to respect their dad. Help them develop love for their siblings. Diligently model the joy of living for Christ to your children. Discipline them with love, and be the best mother you can be. Your children are a gift from God. Treasure them.

While you and your husband are faithfully ministering to other families in the church, don't forget that your first responsibility is to your own family members.

> These words that I am giving you today are to be in your heart. Repeat them to your children. Talk about them when you sit in your house and when you walk along the road, when you lie down and when you get up. Bind them as a sign on your hand and let them be a symbol on your forehead. Write them on the doorposts of your house and on your gates. (Deut. 6:6–9)

Your children do not need a buddy; they need a mother. Don't be pressured by the lost world to sacrifice your children to ungodly choices. Stand tall on moral issues. Help your children learn to choose friends wisely and to prioritize life correctly. Teach your daughter to dress and behave modestly, and teach your son to be a gentleman. Set appropriate parameters for teens. Create fun family traditions that honor God. Don't leave your children to parent themselves.

Here's a small example. Our son's ball team rescheduled an important makeup game for a Sunday morning. He respectfully let the coach know he couldn't play in that game. Not only did the coach reschedule the game, but he also brought the entire team to worship at our church! The results may not always be so thrilling, but God will always bless His children who obey Him.

Take your parenting skills directly from God's Word, and you can't go wrong.

> Choose for yourselves today the one you will worship.
> . . . As for me and my family, we will worship the LORD.
> (Josh. 24:15)

GIVE THEM A FOUNDATION

Scripture demands that we teach our children God's Word. Children learn by observing, so conscientiously live out your faith in front of them daily. According to Deuteronomy 6, there are four times when you should teach your children God's Word.

1. When you sit at home
2. When you walk
3. When you lie down
4. When you get up

Additionally, we are to repeat them, talk about them, and keep His Word visible before our children. The Hebrew word translated *repeat* means to "sharpen."

Well, that about covers it. God wants us diligently to teach His Word to our children. Notice in verse 6 that this process begins with you, as you have hidden His words in your own heart. You're training up your child to be able to make decisions on his or her own. When your children grow up and leave for college or work, God's Word will remain in their hearts.

REAR, NOT REVERE

Be careful that you do not worship your children. Ask yourself this question: Do my children think they are more important to me than my God? Do I ever put children's activities or desires above Him? Do they believe they are more important than my husband? Treasure those children as a wonderful gift from God, keep priorities in perspective, and worship only God.

Believe me! I know that my children are not perfect, and neither are yours. But the responsibility and benefits of Christian parenting are worth the effort.

The following "My Family" form is provided to help you consider the importance of a Christian family. You may substitute "grand-children" for "children" if it's appropriate.

> Every wise woman builds her house, but a foolish one
> tears it down with her own hands. (Prov. 14:1)

My Family

STATEMENT	Always	Sometimes	Rarely
My children (or grandchildren) would say that I respect my husband.			
My children undoubtedly know that God is the priority of my life.			
My children see me studying God's Word.			
My family hears me pray aloud regularly.			
My family knows that I am praying for them daily.			
We take our crises and difficult times to God, as a family, in prayer.			
We praise God as a family when He blesses.			
We intentionally teach our children from God's Word.			
We teach our children how to live for Christ, using the Bible and example.			
Our family priorities point to our God.			
A non-Christian would notice a difference in our family because of Christ.			
My family looks forward to worship in God's house.			
Our children are disciplined firmly and lovingly.			

I help my children discover their spiritual gifts and use them to serve God.			
I model Christian modesty and teach it to my daughter.			
My family hears me say only positive, supportive words about our church.			
My family is an intentional Christian witness to our neighborhood.			
Our family joyfully commits at least a tithe to our church.			
Visitors to our home observe a family committed to Christ.			
You can often hear Christian music in our home.			
We monitor television, radio music, and computer usage in our home.			
We live within the income God has provided for us.			
Our home is a bright, shining light for our God.			
Visible signs in our home show we belong to God, i.e. Scripture, symbols, etc.			
My family does not hear me speak evil of others.			

The Deacon's House

Work hard to make your home a place of comfort and joy. Create traditions. Laugh together. Enjoy family mealtime. Attempt to set a home atmosphere that will honor God. And use your home for Christian hospitality.

Before we begin our chat about your home, please complete this assignment.

My Home

Using a separate piece of paper, number 1 to 6 and answer these questions.

1. Approximate age of your home: ____

2. Approximate square feet (size of home): _____

3. Furnishings: ❑ New ❑ Nice ❑ Old

4. Decor: ❑ Tres Chic ❑ Nice ❑ Shabby chic

5. Cleanliness:
   ❑ Eat-off-the-floor clean
   ❑ Clean but cluttered
   ❑ Danger alert

6. My cooking expertise:
   ❑ Five-star chef ❑ Conscientious cook ❑ Burned toast

After you have completed the home evaluation quiz, hold the test page in front of you, and tear the page down the middle. You have just demonstrated an important fact. Whether you live in a one-room apartment or a twenty-room mansion, whether your home is decorated like a designer or a fishing lodge, and whether you're a super chef or a hamburger-helper diva is not the point. Scripture instructs us to "practice hospitality." There are oodles of ways you can be hospitable, but we'll concentrate this discussion on ways you can use your home to influence others for Christ.

> Don't neglect to show hospitality, for by doing this some have welcomed angels as guests without knowing it. (Heb. 13:2)

> Pursue hospitality. (Rom. 12:13)

> If she has . . . shown hospitality . . . (1 Tim. 5:10)

> Be hospitable to one another without complaining. (1 Pet. 4:9)

> I was a stranger, and you invited me into your home. (Matt. 25:35 NLT)

When people walk into your home for the first time, do they know you're a Christian by just looking around? When two repairmen were working in our home recently, a Scripture plaque on our wall opened an opportunity to talk about God and invite them to our church. Try this exercise.

Silent Witness Exercise

Begin at your front door. Walk through the living areas of your home and write down every item that might give a clue that you are a Christian (decor, books, symbols, etc.). List them here:

_____

_____

_____

_____

_____

_____

_____

_____

_____

Interior designer Georg Anderson wrote a book titled *Silent Witness*, asserting that Christians can share a witness through their home decor. You may be surprised how often a plumber, a realtor, or guests in your home will ask a question about your beliefs because of a visual witness.

A deacon wife who sees her home as a tool to use for God will greatly multiply her ministry opportunities. How have you used your home for God recently? Complete the form on the next page.

Ways I've Used My Home for Ministry

❏ Invited first-time church guest to my home.
❏ Hosted someone overnight for my church, i.e., missionary, preacher, visiting choir, etc.
❏ Invited new church members to my home for fellowship.
❏ Invited friends from church for fellowship.
❏ Hosted a church gathering (i.e., Sunday school fellowship, small-group meeting, youth party).
❏ Used my home as a witness for Christ to my neighbors.
❏ Other: _____

One deacon couple in our church regularly made their home a hangout for church youth. Others have hosted weekly Bible studies, annual usher cookouts, children's swim parties, or women's teas. Many used their homes to get to know neighbors and share Christ, such as hosting a Christmas tea to share a witness or inviting neighbors for lunch. Another often hosted their children's ball team celebrations and talked with parents about attending church. One hosted a different couple for coffee each Sunday evening after worship services. If we ever needed a place for a missionary or summer intern to stay overnight or over the summer, one deacon and his wife accommodated them. When we were planting a church, one of our deacons and his wife invited almost every first-time guest to their home for Sunday lunch and spent the afternoon convincing them to join us in our endeavor! A deacon and his wife planned an annual potluck Thanksgiving meal for single adults in our church. One planned an annual high tea for the senior adult women at church. Another hosted Christian book reviews as an outreach. Need I go on? Do you get the picture?

If you have children living at home, practice Christian hospitality with their friends. Show love. Model Christianity. Seek opportunities to teach, witness, share, and love them. Our children had permission to volunteer our home for school groups, team events, or as a meeting place. In preschool years we planned playtimes and yard sprinkler parties. During elementary school they were allowed to bring a friend home from class each Thursday if they desired. We planned wonderful birthday parties each year, and one goal of each party was to mention our family's commitment to Christ. During high school one of our sons brought his entire band drum line to our home to hang out once each week. Our daughter's high school drama team came to our home for improv nights monthly. We hosted youth Bible studies, backyard vacation Bible schools, and impromptu gatherings. We used our home as a Christian witness through ball team gatherings, sleepovers, end-of-school celebrations, and holiday celebrations. Work hard to make your home welcoming to your children's friends. Your influence and witness will grow exponentially. Don't miss the opportunity to use your home to influence them and their parents for Christ.

How can you use your home to impact your church and your world for Christ? Look at your stage of life, your sphere of influence, and your interests. Watch for opportunities to practice hospitality and honor God with your home. It does belong to Him, after all.

Simple Hospitality Tips

- Holidays offer an easy excuse for hospitality. How about a backyard Easter egg hunt, a July 4 fireworks viewing, a Christmas caroling party, a New Year's Day morning brunch, etc.?
- Purchase a freezer. Keep frozen soups, casseroles, or cookie dough for ministry and last-minute hospitality opportunities.
- Keep a party box stocked with balloons, crepe paper, party plates and napkins, confetti, and "congratulations" and "happy birthday" signs.
- On the top shelf of your pantry, keep a bag with ingredients for one meal, such as five-can chili.
- Select one great menu with entrée, salad, side dishes, and dessert that you enjoy preparing. Feel free to repeat it for various guests.
- Pretty dishes and napkins make food taste better.
- A standing menu may simplify entertaining. For example, our family ate nachos every Sunday evening after church. It was simple to invite guests to join us for our evening snack.
- Plan an annual event, and do it well. Example: your annual New Year's Eve party, Christmas tea, or last-day-of-school celebration.

- Teach your children to be good hosts. From greeting at the front door to conversing with adults, help your kids learn the joy of sharing their home.
- Entertain purposefully. Jesus said, "Whatever you did for one of the least of these brothers of mine, you did for me" (Matt. 25:40). When you entertain, do it "as unto the Lord." Always give a Christian witness.
- Include single adults in your guest list. Widows, single young adults, and men or women whose spouses travel for business or military service will appreciate Christian fellowship.
- Be famous for some dish, such as chili or brownies. Serve it often.
- We bought a full-sized popcorn popper. Instant party!

Are you nervous about hosting people in your home? Try this tip: Make every guest in your home feel like the most important person in the world. If you can do that, you will succeed in hospitality.

⤙ 4 ⤚

The D Word

Mid-book Quiz

Review instructions from God's Word for wives of deacons:

"Wives, too must be w_____ of _____,
not _____, s_____-_____,
f_____ in e_____" (1 Tim. 3:11).

What Is the D Word?

— — — — — — — — — — —

It was at the top of her shopping list as we strolled through Wal-Mart: *one pink pig*. My college-age daughter, Autumn, worked with middle-school girls at her church, and their mother-daughter sleepover was coming up soon. The theme Scripture was Proverbs 11:22:

> Like a gold ring in a pig's snout
> is a beautiful woman who shows no discretion.
> (Prov. 11:22 NIV)

Autumn attached a gold earring through that stuffed pig's nose and taught from God's Word about the importance of discretion. The pink pig with the gold ring became the mascot for her middle-school girls' class, gently reminding them of the need for Christian purity, harmony, and self-control.

So there it is. The D word: *discretion*. The lack of discretion can damage a deacon wife's ministry effectiveness and that of her husband. She may be sensitive, hardworking, and sincere; but if her blouse is cut too low, a lack of *discretion* overrides good intentions. You and I have both known deacon wives who were amazingly gifted with caring deeds but whose effectiveness was negated by their inattention to parenting or their reputation as gossips. God's Word describes a deacon wife as respectable, faithful, self-controlled, and not a malicious talker—all qualities involving discretion.

You are a woman of discretion, dear deacon wife, or your church would not have selected your husband as a deacon. So this chapter is strictly a refresher course, a quick reminder of this important part of Christian character.

Self-Control

Self-control is one required characteristic stated in 1 Timothy 3:11 for a deacon wife. Self-control is not a one-time decision. It is a day-by-day, minute-by-minute decision, a recurring choice, a developed habit. Which issues of self-control tempt you? For some people alcohol or drugs are not a temptation, but their temper is out of control. Every area of our lives must be controlled by God. Consider the short list of self-control on the next page and underline those areas where you consistently practice self-control.

Self-Controlled?

Temper   Spending   Eating
Habits   Gossip
Language
Dress   Media
Time Management
Patience   Chocolate

(Ooops! I couldn't resist adding chocolate to that list!) Your self-control issue may not be on the list. What area of your life lacks self-control?

I've heard more than one pastor bemoan a serious problem with modesty among their deacon wives or deacons' children. Here's a clue: If you are wondering if a particular item of clothing is modest, it's probably not! God's instruction for modesty applies to every Christian woman, whether she's eight or eighty and whether her measurements are 36-24-36 or 50-50-50. As a Christian woman, you should look your best. After all, you represent your Father God to a lost world, and you are an example for younger Christian women to emulate. Be certain, however, that there is never a question about modesty in your demeanor or your wardrobe. Read 1 Timothy 2:9 below and initial here. ____

> Women are to dress themselves in modest clothing.
> (1 Tim. 2:9)

I once heard a woman commenting about her explosive temper. "That's just the way I am!" she said. God expects us to use self-control in every area of life. Perhaps your self-control issues deal with spending or eating or attitudes. Some women have problems with controlling their time or their tongue or their thoughts.

You and God are aware of every self-control issue in your life. Ask Him to give you strength and wisdom consistently to exercise self-control in each area of your life.

Slander

Webster's Definition

Slander

(n) Words falsely spoken that damage the reputation of another; the act of defaming.

(v) Charge falsely or with malicious intent; attack the good name or reputation of someone.

Am I a Gossip?

Circle Yes or No:

When there is a problem in church, do women run to me to get the "scoop"?   Yes   No

Do I ever begin a sentence with "Don't tell anyone, but . . ."?   Yes   No

Do I ever whisper in public?   Yes   No

If every word I muttered were printed on the local newspaper's front page or broadcast on radio, would it honor God?   Yes   No

---

You have a reputation. You are known as a woman who speaks blessings or as a woman who speaks maliciously, as a person who listens to gossip or one who squelches it.

The issue of malicious talk, or gossip, must be an important one. Paul specifically stated that deacon wives are not to be "malicious talkers" (1 Tim. 3:11 NIV). It's mentioned in Scripture more than one hundred times. Malicious talk looks bad on any Christian, but it can destroy a deacon wife's effectiveness. Over the years I've observed more deacon wives marred by gossip than any other problem.

> But let none of you suffer as a murderer, or as a thief, or
> as an evildoer, or as a busybody in other men's matters.
> (1 Pet. 4:15 KJV)

Plenty of small people enjoy nothing more than belittling another person, critiquing a pastor, or stirring up strife among the believers. A deacon wife should be involved and informed. She should pray without ceasing. But being a busybody is a sin.

> No rotten talk should come from your mouth, but only
> what is good for the building up of someone in need, in
> order to give grace to those who hear. (Eph. 4:29)

First Peter 4:15 lists that sin right in the same list with murderers, thieves, and evildoers. This is serious! That same word is translated "meddler" in the Holman Christian Standard Version, and the New Living Translation calls it "prying into other people's affairs." Whatever you call it, don't do it.

> But, as the One who called you is holy, you also are to
> be holy in all your conduct; for it is written, Be holy,
> because I am holy. (1 Pet. 1:15–16)

Juicy details about someone's life, even if it's disguised as a "prayer request," are still gossip. Have you ever been in a Bible class or prayer meeting where every vivid detail of an illness was spelled out? Or private affairs were laid public in a pretense of concern? When people ask you to pray for them, that does not give you permission to plaster their needs for public view. There is a fine line between gossip and prayer requests.

True story: I'd cultivated her friendship and invited her to my church for two long years, and my coworker Jan showed up for Sunday school one Sunday. I was ecstatic! After her Bible class I walked with her toward the worship service. She whispered, "Diana, you should've *warned* me about that." The class she attended was nothing more than a gossip session. The women had spent most of the time listing in sordid detail every personal problem or physical ailment of every person they knew. A few brief moments of Bible class were dedicated to a token jab at God's Word. *Jan never came back to our church.*

Maybe you don't truly intend to gossip. Dear deacon wife, your small words count big. I know it sounds corny, but it's malicious if you simply demean Mrs. Jones's lopsided cake. It's gossip, even if it's about children. One must not repeat negative details of another person's life, injury, mistakes, or marriage.

> LORD, set up a guard for my mouth; keep watch at the door of my lips. (Ps. 141:3)

> I said, "I will guard my ways so that I may not sin with my tongue; I will guard my mouth with a muzzle as long as the wicked are in my presence." (Ps. 39:1)

> Your speech should always be gracious, seasoned with salt, so that you may know how you should answer each person. (Col. 4:6)

Remember this: your God-given purpose in life is *not* to keep everyone else *informed*. Rather than informing others, get busy praying for the need. Minister to people in a tangible way. Encourage them, but don't talk about them.

It takes two to gossip. By merely listening to gossip, you participate in the sin as much as the gossiper, so decide ahead of time how you will respond. How can a woman halt gossip when someone talks maliciously to her?

During a funeral service a friend of the deceased made this statement: "I never heard her say a bad word about anyone." Could that be said at *your* funeral? A deacon wife should strive to make that a legacy in her life. Don't gossip.

Your reputation for positive words will increase ministry opportunities and effectiveness. Other women in the church will come to trust you with a problem or a confidence. Bottom line: think before you speak. Honor God with every word.

> For the mouth speaks from the overflow of the heart.
> (Matt. 12:34)

Tips to Avoid Malicious Speech

- It takes two to gossip. If you're *listening*, that makes you number two.
- At the first hint of gossip, immediately interrupt.
- Never whisper. It looks like you're gossiping even if you're not.
- Be polite but don't participate.
- Don't disguise gossip as prayer.
- Your best friend shouldn't be the church gossip.
- Don't allow a person's character to be degraded.

- Correct misinformation.
- Watch your nonverbal responses. A raised eyebrow can equal gossip.
- When sharing prayer requests, don't give too much information. God knows the details.
- Even if you say it to a friend, it's still gossip.
- Never speak negatively about the church down the street.
- Guard what you put in print. It could be taken out of context, may appear more harsh than intended, or may be forwarded to hundreds!
- Just because it's true doesn't mean it's appropriate to verbalize.
- Stop, drop, and pray.

Confidentiality

If a woman in your church had a great need and wanted to ask a Christian woman to pray for her privately, would she confide in you? Dear deacon wife, you must be able to keep a confidence. When a church member trusts you with information, that doesn't mean she wants the whole church to know.

Harmony

I always thought my dad and mom were the model deacon and wife. They committed their lives to serving God and enhancing harmony within their local church. If a church business meeting became argumentative, Dad, a man of few words, would stand and quote a Scripture about harmony. He and Mom would work behind the scenes to put out small fires or disagreements. They had a way of gently calming unneeded dissension in the church. For many years I've observed the priceless value of harmony-enhancing deacons and deacon wives in churches where my husband served as pastor.

Before you read further, reread every word of Acts 6:1–7, a biblical account of a conflict within the early church.

> In those days, as the number of the disciples was multiplying, there arose a complaint by the Hellenistic Jews against the Hebraic Jews that their widows were being overlooked in the daily distribution. Then the Twelve summoned the whole company of the disciples and said, "It would not be right for us to give up preaching about God to wait on tables. Therefore, brothers, select from among you seven men of good reputation, full of the Spirit and wisdom, whom we can appoint to this duty. But we will devote ourselves to prayer and to the preaching ministry." The proposal pleased the whole company. So they chose Stephen, a man full of faith and the Holy Spirit, and Philip, Prochorus, Nicanor, Timon, Parmenas, and Nicolaus, a proselyte from Antioch. They had them stand before the apostles, who prayed and laid their hands on them.
>
> So the preaching about God flourished, the number of disciples in Jerusalem multiplied greatly, and a large group of priests became obedient to the faith. (Acts 6:1–7)

Many Bible scholars believe this to be the account of the first deacon selection. Here's the setting: There was trouble in the church.

There were rumblings that some of the widows weren't receiving a fair portion in the daily distribution of food. Conflict.

The disciples summoned the church members and said, "It would not be right for us to give up preaching about God to wait on tables." They challenged the church to select seven men who had wisdom, a good reputation, and were full of the Spirit, and appoint them to that duty. The word used for "wait on tables" is the Greek word *deaconizo* from which we get our word *deacon*. When those seven men began to assist with the problem, the disciples could continue to devote themselves to prayer and the preaching ministry (v. 4).

It was a win-win situation. The plan pleased the entire church. The complainers were appeased, the widows were cared for, and the prayer and preaching ministry of the leaders was uninterrupted. The men in this passage were not called as a board of directors or administrators for the apostles. They were called to assist the church leaders with ministry in the church family, to solve church problems, to be servant leaders.

As in any family, conflicts may arise occasionally. The church in Jerusalem experienced conflict about allowing Gentiles into the church. Paul addressed conflict with the church in Philippi, Corinth, and Ephesus. When conflict arises, deacons must act with dignity. As they lovingly "step up to the plate" to calm adversity and help with the problem, their wives can also assist with peacemaking.

Now here's the best part of the story. The very next verse, verse 7, states that after that complaint was resolved the number of disciples multiplied greatly! The church not only grew; it *multiplied greatly*! Deacons, as servant leaders, can help set the church growth pattern by enhancing harmony.

I was a member of the same church for most of my childhood and teen years. Steve and I had arrived to meet with the pastor for pre-marital counseling. Before he began our session, he told us a story:

I know that God has called you to pastor, Steve, and I pray that during your years of ministry, you'll have a deacon like your future father-in-law. I believe that he probably saved my ministry at one point.

There was a very heated debate during a deacon's meeting at our church one day. Darris was highly respected among the deacons. He had listened quietly, but when the debate became out of control, he stood slowly and said, "Men, we are deacons in this church, and we are not going to behave in this manner." The explosive atmosphere calmed immediately, and there was harmony in that group afterward.

That pastor went on to serve in the church for decades of effective ministry and retired in that community, a loved and effective minister.

Robert Naylor, in his book *The Baptist Deacon,* said it this way: "When a man becomes a deacon, he loses the privilege, if such exists, of participating in a church row [controversy or disagreement]."

It was the cutest thing! When Steve and I led a national conference for deacons and deacon wives at Ridgecrest and Glorieta LifeWay Conference Centers, he gave each deacon two buckets to carry around everywhere they went for the entire week. One bucket was labeled with a big W and the second one had a big G. Steve told those deacons that every deacon carries two buckets: one filled with water and the other filled with gasoline. When a church fire, or problem, arises, it is a deacon's responsibility to pour water on that problem, not gas!

Each deacon proudly carried his buckets all around campus that week. When asked about the buckets, the deacons explained the problem-solving responsibility of deacons in the church. Over and over the deacons told the story of Acts 6, the problem with food distribution in that growing church, and the selection of deacons to alleviate the problem and restore church harmony. Over and over they were reminded of their enormous responsibility to enhance peace and multiply ministry within their own churches. When faced with a church problem (a fire), they should douse it with water, not spread it with gas.

How will you, a deacon's wife, respond to a problem within the church family? Will you hide? Or shush? Or run? Or add fuel? Believe it or not, ladies, your influence and reaction can greatly impact peace-making in your church family. If you'll reread your "job description" as a deacon's wife (1 Tim. 3:11), you'll be inspired to make a positive difference during church conflict. Watch out for sparks!

HARMONY LESSONS

Let's look at some practical tips to help deacon wives enhance harmony.

Listen. Let's face it, a deacon wife has a "pew view." One pastor described it like this: "A deacon wife helps by being another set of spiritual eyes and ears upon the needs of the congregation." You often hear grumblings even before the pastor! When you hear complaining within your circle of influence, you have three choices: join in, clam up, or help with the solution, throwing water on the problem. How will you respond? (Clue: there's a W on your bucket.)

> Brothers, do not complain about one another, so that you will not be judged. Look, the judge stands at the door! (James 5:9)

> I pour out my complaint before Him [God]; I reveal my trouble to Him. (Ps. 142:2)

> Do everything without grumbling and arguing. (Phil. 2:14)

Choose your friends. A deacon wife should probably not be best friends with the church gossip or complainer. You know who they are, and so does the rest of the church. Love them, be kind to them, and minister to them. But don't be best friends with them.

> Do not be deceived: "Bad company corrupts good morals." (1 Cor. 15:33)

> The one who walks with the wise will become wise, but a companion of fools will suffer harm. (Prov. 13:20)

Respond carefully. When gossip or complaining occurs, silence is not always golden. Your nonresponse to a complaint or gossip may be taken as agreement. It takes two to gossip—one to talk and one to listen. When you hear grumblings, lovingly squelch them flat. Say a silent prayer to ask for God's wisdom and then respond.

Watch your eyebrows. Women in the church are watching to see how you react to a problem or controversy. Be careful of your verbal and nonverbal responses to problems.

Make a plan. A complaining woman is often simply uninformed or uninvolved. Invite her for coffee and talk about God's blessings on your church. Minister to her. Pray aloud for her. Invite her to help you with a ministry project. You don't know every detail of her life, but God does. Just love her.

> Don't criticize one another. (James 4:11)

Never be part of the problem. Think about it. If a deacon is busy serving and enhancing harmony but his wife is stirring up gossip or causing trouble in a business meeting, what has been accomplished? As the wife of a deacon, you have given up any right, if there ever was such a right, to fan flames of discontent in God's church. No exceptions.

Be part of the solution. Exercise self-control. Be respectable. Be faithful in all things. Don't slander. (Do those four instructions sound familiar?) Weigh each word you speak. Lovingly squelch gossip flat. Pray before you respond wisely. Forgive. Show love and peace with your words and actions. Show support for your pastor and pastor's wife. Always point the offended to a healthy resolution.

Encourage your husband. When there is a harmony problem in the church, the burden may be heavy for him. Don't nag or instruct. Pray, and let him know you are praying. Trust that God will give him wisdom as he assists the pastor to restore church harmony.

Help carry the load. An ostrich with its head in the sand doesn't solve many problems. Pay attention to needs around you. The load of ministry doesn't stop when the church is in turmoil. Find needs and meet them. Be faithful in attendance. Make a hospital visit. Send a note to a bereaved member. Call guests who visited your church last Sunday.

Be joyful. Remember that God cares deeply about His bride, the church, and He is in control. Today's problems are no surprise to Him. Confidence in Him will produce joy.

Read the Instruction Book. Much of the New Testament is written about harmony. Stay in the Word, and your commitment to harmony will increase.

Pray. You already know from personal experience that prayer changes things. When there is a harmony problem in the church, make a commitment to pray like you've never prayed before. The God of the universe is listening, and He cares more about your church than you. Perhaps you will decide to go to the church building each morning, kneel at the altar, and spend time asking God to protect your church family. You may fast and pray. You may pray aloud with your husband daily during crisis times in the church.

Some don'ts for church conflict. Don't read or write anonymous letters. Don't hate. Don't act like you have all the answers. Don't belittle. Don't fret. Don't be the source. Don't spread rumors. Don't hold a grudge. Don't retaliate. Don't forget that God's in control.

When I was a girl, I sang in the Texas Girls Choir. We often sang a cappella. Did you know that just one voice singing off-key can ruin the sound of an entire choir? Disharmony is not a pretty sound. Likewise in God's church—a church without harmony dishonors God. Remember, it doesn't take a lot of musical ability to harp about something.

Do your part to watch out for sparks, dear deacon wives.

How Will You Help Keep Harmony in Your Church?

❏ Read God's Word.
❏ Listen with love.
❏ Choose friends wisely.
❏ Watch my nonverbal communication.
❏ Be part of the solution.
❏ Encourage my husband.
❏ Help carry the load.
❏ Be joyful.
❏ Pray.

Can You Name . . .

Four characteristics of a deacon wife from 1 Timothy?

1. W_____ of R_____

2. Not _____

3. S____-_____

4. F_____ ____ _____
1 Timothy ____ : ____

⇢ 5 ⇠

Ministry Tips

When I was growing up, I watched my mother, a deacon wife, as she joyfully used her talents in our church. Ministering to others in our church was a part of her everyday lifestyle. She taught teenage girls in Sunday school for decades. She loved giving bridal and baby showers for church members. She thrived on inviting Christians to our home for fellowship. I can remember many times when she prepared a meal for the family of a hospital patient or a bereaved family. She helped with church outreach and special church projects.

Oh, she was certainly busy with her family of six, her full-time job, and her many other responsibilities; but she never seemed burdened or perturbed by opportunities to serve God. Our family's needs were not neglected because of her activity at the church alongside my dad. My brothers and sister and I were proud of our parents' commitment. We were included and involved with our parents as they joyfully served God.

Dear deacon wife, you probably have no idea what an impact your ministry will make. You represent Jesus Christ. You represent His bride, the church. You represent your pastor and your deacon husband. Your ministry is a reminder of God's love demonstrated

97

through His church. Any Christian woman has opportunities to show love to church family members, but as the wife of a deacon, your opportunities will multiply.

Get Ready

In the Southern Baptist Convention, each church is totally autonomous (self-governed), so deacon ministries are accomplished in a wide variety of ways. Some churches assign specific families to deacons for ministry. Others divide church members for ministry by address, Bible study classes, or age. Some churches use a team approach, capitalizing on each deacon's gifts and interests. Still other churches use a rotation system with different deacons "on call." Many churches encourage the wives of their deacons to assist them in ministering to families. If half of your church congregation is female, there may be many times when you can make a connection that would be more personal because you are a woman. It is imperative that you joyfully follow your church's guidelines.

Consider these needs and crises that may happen within the church family:

Death	Bereavement	Elderly parent
Marital problems	Divorce	Relocation
Loss of home	Community disaster	Sickness
Loneliness	Hurt feelings	Job termination
Apathy	Depression	Hospitalization
Financial problem	Suicide	Graduation
New Christian	Terminal illness	New job
Marriage	Aging Parent	Problem child
New baby	New home	Addictions

And that's just a starter list! Opportunities abound for you to show God's love and care to church family members. Within your sphere of influence, you may be the first to hear of a need or problem. Listen carefully, inform the church office appropriately, and do your best to help meet needs. Ask God to give you discernment and awareness of how He would have you serve.

As a pastor's wife, I can assure you that it's not possible to accomplish all the ministries needed without deacons and their wives. Deacons and deacon wives in our church are invaluable. As you help carry the load, your church and God's kingdom will benefit.

In this chapter we'll address some general guidelines to help a deacon wife be prepared for ministry opportunities, and some specific suggestions for a few types of hands-on ministry. (You can find hundreds of other ministry ideas in my first book, *Fresh Ideas—1,000 Ways to Grow a Thriving and Energetic Church*.) Your church field is unique. Adjust or expand these suggestions to fit your own mission field.

> Foolish man! Are you willing to learn that faith without works is useless? (James 2:20)

> Serve wholeheartedly, as if you were serving the Lord, not men. (Eph. 6:7 NIV)

Get Set

By preparing ahead of time, a deacon wife's effectiveness in ministering can be enhanced. A few tips:

In preparation for ministry, a deacon's wife may want to order personal "business" cards, printing her name and contact information. An investment of just a few dollars will buy a box of a thousand cards, and you'll be amazed at the ways you will use these for ministry. Some deacon wives select a lovely color or graphic design. Others add a favorite Scripture at the bottom or print the plan of salvation on the reverse side. It's not necessary to print "deacon wife" on the card unless that is your preference. Use them freely, jotting a note on the back when a hospital patient is away for tests, writing the room number for a Bible class for a church guest, or leaving a card as you make outreach visits.

Purchase a small-sized Bible or a *Share Jesus without Fear* New Testament that will fit in your handbag. You will be surprised how often God will open a door for you to read or share His Word.

A deacon wife can further prepare herself for ministry by gathering appropriate Scripture references for various situations. As you read your Bible, make notes of favorite Scriptures. Watch for Scriptures you might use in specific ministry settings, such as suicide, long-term illness, crisis situation, or marital difficulty. Print Scriptures on adhesive paper to fit inside your purse Bible. Although you may have those Scriptures memorized, this tangible list may assist you in a crisis moment. (See Scriptures below.)

Quick Reference Scriptures for Ministry Visits

Psalm 91	God's protection in danger
Psalm 23	Comfort
Psalm 103	God's mercy
John 3:16	For God so loved the world . . .
Psalm 23:4	God is with me
1 Corinthians 13	Love
Romans 8:18	What we suffer now
Psalm 116:15	Precious is the death of saints

Matthew 5:4	Blessed are they who mourn
Romans 8:31	If God is for us
Isaiah 66:13	I will comfort you
Psalm 73:26	My flesh may fail, but God
Romans 8:28	All things work together
John 14:1–6	Let not your heart be troubled
Philippians 4:6–7	Don't be anxious
Revelation 14:13	Blessed/die in the Lord
Job 19:25	My Redeemer lives
Romans 12:12	Patient in affliction, joy, pray
Proverbs 3:5–6	Trust God, lean
2 Corinthians 4:16	Renew day by day
2 Timothy 1:12	I know whom I have believed
Revelation 21:1–7	Heaven
Isaiah 41:10, 13	Don't be afraid
1 Peter 5:7	Cast your care on Him
2 Corinthians 5:1–8	This earthly tent
2 Timothy 4:6–8	Fought the good fight
1 Corinthians 15:54–55	Death, where is your sting
John 10:27–29	My sheep hear My voice
Matthew 6:9–13	Lord's Prayer
John 11:25–26	I am the resurrection and life
Romans 8:35–39	Can anything separate us
2 Corinthians 12:7–10	His grace is sufficient
Matthew 11:28–30	Come to Me, you weary
1 Thessalonians 4:13–17	When Christians die

In your personal date book or cell phone memory, write the church phone number and the home and cell phone numbers for your pastor's wife and one or two other deacon wives. When an emergency occurs, you can quickly ask for help or for prayer. If you have a favorite area of ministry, such as homebound members, keep that phone or e-mail list in a convenient location, too.

Prepare for ministry by using your talents and interests. For example, if you love gardening, plant roses or zinnias and take fresh flowers when you make ministry visits. If you love scrapbooking or crafts, prepare Scripture bookmarks or cards to use for ministry visits or notes. One deacon wife in our church loved ceramics, and she made personalized ceramic booties with a Scripture for every newborn in our church. Another loved to shop online. She purchased several dozen guest books to use for ministry. She was often the first guest when a church member arrived for an extended hospital stay, and she delivered that guest book as an encouragement for the patient.

Develop good personal habits to enhance ministry. The simple act of making eye contact makes a difference whether you're delivering a flower on a widow's birthday, welcoming a newcomer at church, or making an outreach visit. By looking directly into a person's eyes, you convey your sincere interest and concern.

Be ready to be inconvenienced for the sake of ministry. Timeliness counts. Ministry opportunities are often time sensitive. A crisis is never planned, and effective ministry must often occur quickly. An immediate visit or telephone call or a carefully timed note or card can increase its impact. For example, if your ministry is to hold her hand during the surgery of a loved one, that can only be accomplished during the surgery. Although an urgent situation may occur at an inconvenient time for you personally, it's worth the effort to respond in a timely manner.

Your ministry effectiveness will be more effective when you call a person by name. If you're not great at remembering names, try these ideas. Keep an index card in your Bible or bag and write an ongoing list of names—new acquaintances, guests at church, church members, etc. Refer to your list before entering church on Sunday. Attempt to learn children's and teens' names, too. When you meet newcomers at church, repeat their name in conversation at least twice. Keep a church directory near the phone and inside your car to check names before making visits. Most importantly, when praying with someone, mention the person by name.

Go!

As a deacon wife learns of needs within the church, she should do whatever ministry she can to help and keep the church staff informed. For example, when a member of her Bible class calls about a death in her family, the deacon wife will immediately make a call to be certain that the church office, pastor, and Sunday school teacher are informed. She may offer to go to the member's home to assist with making notification calls or to help her prepare for guests. She may call the pastor's wife to see if she's available to accompany her to deliver a cake or stop by the home for prayer.

Pray that God will make you aware of many opportunities to minister to church members in need. Needs in your church are unique, but a few starter ideas are provided below.

> Therefore, my dear brothers, be steadfast, immovable,
> always excelling in the Lord's work, knowing that your
> labor in the Lord is not in vain. (1 Cor. 15:58)

BEREAVEMENT

One of the primary opportunities of ministry for deacon wives in our church occurred when a church member or friend or relative of a church member died. Deacon wives often went to the home to help relatives with telephone notification of friends and relatives. They sometimes answered the door for the grieving family or helped with drinks and food for incoming relatives. They helped with transportation, babysitting, pet sitting, and a variety of trivial details. One deacon wife was sent to purchase clothing for two grandchildren to wear for the funeral. Occasionally they would help with a discrete quick cleaning of the grieving member's living room. Often a deacon wife's most important act of ministry was her presence. Our deacon wives organized a meal for the grieving family after funerals. They had ministered in this way many times and had developed a great system. Our deacon wives made a significant Christian impact on every grieving person in our church, joyfully and respectfully serving in a time of need.

Send a monthly note to a bereaved widow or family member for a year to eighteen months after a death. A deacon and wife could deliver a recording of the funeral service a month after the funeral. A short telephone call to check on the bereaved will be appreciated. Show love during difficult days.

She's Lonely

A woman at your church seems lonely. What can you do?

- Learn her name.
- Wear your name tag.
- Listen.
- Sit near her.
- Watch for her.
- Introduce her to others with similar interests.
- Help her find a place of involvement at church.
- Help her find a ministry at church.
- Help her meet someone at church who lives near her.
- Pray for her.

SICKNESS

Visiting the sick—it's part of being a servant of Christ! When speaking of the sick, Jesus said, "I assure you: Whatever you did for one of the least of these brothers of Mine, you did for Me" (Matt. 25:40). As a deacon wife you may help organize meals or child care. You may take an evening shift at the hospital or sit with family members during surgery. Long-term illness or extended recovery time can offer special opportunities to show God's love. There are innumerable ways you can show God's love to the sick. Try some of these:

Freeze soup. A deacon wife may keep frozen containers of homemade soup or casseroles ready for ministry in times of sickness. I often kept an extra batch of homemade cookie dough, labeled "ministry cookies," in our freezer. You'd be surprised how often an opportunity will arise to minister in His name when you're prepared for it.

Fit the need. If she's broken her leg, purchase an inexpensive cane at the drugstore, ask deacons and church staff and friends to use permanent markers to autograph it and draw Scripture art, and then give her a special blessing! If she's had wisdom teeth removed, drop by with a giant ice drink or a milk shake. If she's confined to bed during pregnancy, bring her crochet needles and thread and a pattern for baby booties.

Give a puzzle photo. Take a digital photo of a group of people in your church who care about the patient such as their Bible class or a group of deacons and wives. E-mail the photo to a puzzle company, such as www.puzzles.com to create a wonderful jigsaw puzzle. They can add word bubbles above a few people, such as "I miss you most," "Get well soon, Nelda," or "If you don't get well soon, we'll have Sunday school at your house!"

Plan a progressive floral arrangement. Here's a fun project for a group of deacon wives. One deacon's wife visits a hospitalized church member to deliver a vase containing a sparse arrangement of flowers. Other deacon wives are scheduled to stop by every hour that day, delivering a few more flowers from their garden or florist to create a lovely bouquet.

Personalize a pillowcase. For a thoughtful gift during a long-term hospital stay, members of your class, church, or deacon body can sign their names in permanent marker on a bright yellow pillowcase, adding art, Scripture, encouraging words, and funny notes.

You're not forgotten. When a member has a long-term illness, mail a get-well card weekly or monthly.

Send one-a-day blessings. Distribute get-well cards to deacon wives to write a personal note of encouragement. Collect the cards, and mail one every day. Alternately, ask each deacon wife to sign one large get-well card, cut it into jigsaw puzzle shapes, and mail a few pieces each day for the patient to assemble.

Provide one-a-day treats. A long-term illness can be brightened if you deliver a basket of small, individually wrapped gifts and notes. Tell her to open one each day to remind her of God's love and your prayers.

Borrow this! When a church member was bedfast for several months, our deacon wives prepared a lovely basket full of "on-loan" books and videos.

Curb loneliness. Once she's feeling better but still housebound, ask if you can bring dinner (home cooked, store-bought, or picnic) and leisurely dine together.

Text message a prayer reminder. If the patient uses a cell phone, send an occasional text message to remind her of your prayers.

Send prayer grams. Print an attractive card labeled "Prayer Gram," leaving plenty of room for a personal note to be added. Distribute copies to her Bible class or other friends, collect the notes, and mail them in one big envelope.

Take this. Deliver a church bulletin along with a recording of last

Sunday's sermon or Bible study. You could include a recording of the Bible study group singing a funny song for the patient. (You can find hundreds of other ministry ideas in my first book, *Fresh Ideas—1,000 Ways to Grow a Thriving and Energetic Church*.)

> I was sick and you took care of Me. (Matt. 25:36)

> Whatever you do, do it enthusiastically, as something done for the Lord and not for men, knowing that you will receive the reward of an inheritance from the Lord—you serve the Lord Christ. (Col. 3:23–24)

HOSPITAL VISITATION

You probably have no idea what an impact your visit to a hospitalized patient will make. Even if you hate hospitals (I do!), it's worth your effort to visit the sick in Jesus' name. You are an ambassador for your God, your church, and your pastor every time you make a hospital visit. Your visit is a reminder to that patient of God's love demonstrated through His church. This is important!

You may sit with a family member during a surgery or grieve with the family of a dying patient. Your ministry to family members may open doors for evangelism or further ministry after the hospitalization. You may sometimes volunteer to sit overnight with a patient to give family members a rest.

A patient who feels well may enjoy an extended afternoon visit to help pass the time. Most hospital visits, however, should be brief. The reason the patient is hospitalized is because she is sick, after all! Be sensitive to each situation. Here's a quickie primer about how to make a hospital visit (reprinted from *Fresh Ideas for Women's Ministry*, B&H, 2008).

> When did we see You sick, or in prison, and visit You? (Matt. 25:39)

How to Make a Hospital Visit

1. Preparation for the visit:
   - Dress appropriately. Do not chew gum or wear perfume. Wear your church name tag. It will help the patient to feel more comfortable.
   - Be aware of hospital rules, such as visiting hours.
   - Consider taking another deacon wife or church staff wife with you.
   - Before you leave your car, pray for God's guidance.
   - Carry a church directory in your car. Glance at it before entering the hospital to help recall family member faces and names.
   - Take your small Bible, a small gift (see below), and a witnessing tract.

2. When you arrive:
   - Wash your hands before entering the room and between visits to patients. There is more danger of passing germs to patients than in getting germs from them.
   - Obey posted notices on the patient's door. If visitors aren't allowed, leave a note with the nurse.
   - Knock softly, wait for an answer, and then enter.
   - As you enter the room, observe details. For example, notice the presence or absence of cards, flowers, and visitors. Silently ask God, *How can You use me to show Your love to this patient?*

3. During the visit:
   - Even if you know the patient well, introduce yourself by name as well as the church name.
   - If the patient is asleep, speak her name softly. (She may

just have her eyes closed.) Leave a note so she will know that you were there.

- Call the patient by name.
- Place yourself sitting or standing in direct line of vision of the patient so she can speak and listen without strain.
- Smile. Be relaxed and cheerful. Look confident. You are God's representative. Never express negative feelings when in the patient's room.
- Never sit on, lean on, or touch the bed. Be polite and stand if there are not enough chairs.
- Never hug. When you pray, it may be appropriate to touch the patient's arm or hand.
- Don't yell. Don't whisper. Talk audibly. Increase your volume if you find the patient cannot hear you.
- Listen more than you talk. Sincerely care, but don't intrude. Don't ask about the diagnosis. Say "We just came by to check on you" instead of "How are you feeling?" Allow the patient to share only if they initiate it. Unless you are a medical professional, do not give medical advice. Do not share stories of your own illnesses or surgeries. Do not discuss others who have had it.
- Do not eat the patient's food, either from his tray or from gifts others have left.
- Use your common sense. Remember that patients are in the hospital because they are sick.
- Always read a verse of Scripture before you leave. Carry a small Bible marked with a favorite appropriate Scripture, and read it before you pray. Write the Scripture reference on your card so she can meditate on it later.
- Pray aloud. Ask, "Would you mind if I pray for you before I leave?" Offer a brief prayer of gratitude and trust.

- Leave something. Any small token will remind the patient of your visit and of God's love shown through you. Need ideas?
  ! Last Sunday's bulletin.
  ! Current church newsletter.
  ! Your personal business card with a note.
  ! A Scripture bookmark.
  ! A flower from your garden.
  ! A card.
  ! A journal or guest book.
  ! A Christian book or CD.
  ! An audio of church friends singing a fun get well song.
  ! A recording of Sunday's sermon.
  ! A photo of her friends at church holding a "God bless you" sign.
  ! Book, magazine, or other reading material.
- Don't overstay. However, don't act hurried or anxious. The most important thing in the world you have to do is be with the person *right now*. A hospital visit will often last about five or ten minutes.

4. Additional ministry opportunities:
   - If a family member needs relief, offer to stay with the patient while they take a break or go home for a quick shower.
   - There may be an occasion when you offer to sit overnight with a patient to relieve a family member.
   - Be very conscious of the patient's roommate and guests. God may give an opportunity to share a witness, leave a tract, or pray for them.
   - Be aware of ministry opportunities with nurses and doctors. Pray for them when you pray for the patient.

5. After the visit:
- As you leave the hospital, stop by the restroom and wash your hands.
- Call or e-mail the church office to inform the pastor of your visit and the patient's condition.
- Confidentiality is essential. Never repeat personal information or medical details.
- If there is a specific need, do your best to assist. If you promise to do something, do it.
- Pray for the patient.
- Drop a note to remind the patient of your prayers.

Matthew 25:40 says, "Whatever you did for one of the least of these brothers of Mine, you did for Me." Jesus spoke these words in relation to demonstrating compassion to the hungry, thirsty, lonely, and sick.

HOMEBOUND VISITS

If members of your church are homebound, consider making occasional or regular visits to see them. Some deacons and deacon wives attempt to visit each homebound member during a year. Others visit a particular homebound member weekly. There may be a homebound member of your church who lives near your home or near your children's school. You may have a relationship with a member who has become homebound.

> Begin a list of homebound members of your church:
>
> _____
>
> _____
>
> _____

Your method of homebound visitation will fit your personality and lifestyle. You may make a quick stop at their front door. You might enjoy a leisurely hour of playing checkers or chatting on the back porch. Here are a few tips to help you get started:

- Call ahead to let her know you'd like to stop by for a visit.
- Wear your church name tag.
- Call her by name.
- As you arrive, observe. Does she raise flowers? Are there photos of family? Evidence of hobbies? Are there obvious needs?
- Even a brief visit will be appreciated.
- Listen more than you talk.
- Smile.
- Laugh together.
- Talk about how God is working in your life and hers.
- Deliver a Christian magazine, such as *Mission Mosaic* or *Journey.*
- Deliver a flower from your garden.
- Deliver a tape or CD of last Sunday's sermon.
- Deliver her Sunday school book quarterly.
- Take a copy of Sunday's bulletin or recent church newsletter.
- Ask about her family and friends.

- If she enjoys reading, deliver a book from the church library each month.
- Before you leave, voice a prayer for her.
- Take photos from the church pageant or picnic to show her.
- On her birthday stop by with streamers, balloons, and a candlelit cupcake.
- Deliver a small seasonal gift such as an Easter lily, valentine candy, Christmas cookies.
- Paint her fingernails.
- Write a letter for her.
- Read the Bible aloud with her. If you read weekly for fifteen minutes, you can complete the entire New Testament in two years.
- Call ahead to tell her you'll bring batteries for her smoke detector and some extra lightbulbs. Take a small stepladder.
- Ask her to tell you about how she came to know Christ.
- Tell her about good things happening at the church.
- Arrive with a portable tea party. In a picnic basket pack a thermos of hot water, tea bags, cookies, and froufrou napkins. Serve her elegantly!
- If you made homemade soup last night, take her a bowl of it.
- Christmas carol at her home with your family or friends. Take an instant photo with her. Deliver a homemade ornament or signed Christmas card.
- Arrange for a children's or adult Sunday school department to "adopt" a homebound member who has no family.

NURSING HOME VISITS

Make a commitment to show God's love to church members in the nursing home. Most suggestions for homebound visits apply here. A few additional ideas:

- If you're good at decorating, ask if you can prepare a seasonal wreath for her room or door. Change it a few times each year.
- If your church plans a nursing home ministry, attempt to arrange it at the home where a church member resides. Let her know ahead of time so she can invite her friends. Churches can work with the home to provide worship services, hymn sing, children's Christmas nativity parade, and regular nursing home visitation by a women's group.
- Get to know those who work at the nursing home. Occasionally bring them a treat. Offer a word of encouragement. Learn their names. Share Christ.

Review for Final Exam

"Wives, too, must be worthy of r_____, not s_____, s_____-c_____ed, f_____ful in everything" (1 Tim. _____:11).

MINISTRY IN THE SUNSHINE

Don't wait for a crisis to minister in your church. Some of your most important impact will occur in everyday situations as you build Christian friendships and show God's love. You'll help with a baby shower or attend a church member's wedding. You'll assist with baptism or celebrate a graduation. You'll help begin a new Sunday school class.

Always be ready to serve others in Christ's name. Watch for opportunities. Many important ministry opportunities only take minutes of your time, but if you aren't alert, you may miss them.

When there is a need in the church, the pastor and members will often look to the deacons and deacon wives for assistance. What an honor! Be the first to volunteer when it is possible. Watch carefully for any opportunity to serve your great God.

Your regular lifestyle as a Christian woman will minister to members of your church. Now that's simple enough, isn't it?

> "God is our refuge and strength, a helper who is always found in times of trouble. Therefore we will not be afraid, though the earth trembles and the mountains topple into the depths of the seas, though its waters roar and foam and the mountains quake with its turmoil. . . . The LORD of Hosts is with us" (Ps. 46:1–3, 7).

CRISIS SITUATIONS

If a disaster hits your church or your community, be ready to "step up to the plate" and minister to others. What could a deacon wife do to help in a tragedy such as a tornado, fire, flood, or hurricane? If a crisis hits your local elementary school, prison, or city hall, will you be ready to show God's love in some way? If a national disaster occurs, will you see the opportunities to minister in His name?

Just after the *Columbia* space shuttle disaster, I was on the search line as a victim chaplain in the woods near Hemphill, Texas. After an exhausting morning, our team of FBI, NASA, firefighters, and emergency workers met the Red Cross truck to have a sack lunch. Inside each lunch was a ziplock bag with a giant homemade cookie and a Scripture note. It was signed, "We're praying for you today. First

Baptist Church." What timing! Deacon wives at that small church had never expected a space shuttle to explode above their community, but when that disaster occurred, they quickly found a way to minister to others. Will you be ready?

PASTORAL TRANSITION

The entire church is waiting expectantly. A pulpit committee has been formed, and as they diligently seek your church's new pastor, you wait. This is not the time to take a nap, dear deacon wife! This is a critical time for your church. How can you help during this interim time?

Encourage the pastor search committee

- Show great interest and support, but avoid probing for information. Trust God.
- Pray faithfully for the committee. Post a note on your dressing table or car visor to remind you to pray. Mail prayer notes to the committee. Ask all the deacon wives to sign a monthly note of prayer and encouragement to the chairman.
- Speak positively about your church and the pulpit committee. Your attitude helps set the pace for a positive interim period.
- Offer to assist with pastor search committee members' church or personal responsibilities when they travel to hear potential pastors. For example, if a committee member teaches third graders, offer to substitute. Volunteer to help with their family obligations.
- Be alert for ways to encourage the committee, such as providing snacks or box lunches for an extended meeting or travel day.

While you're waiting . . .

- Challenges inevitably arise during an interim period.
  Plan ahead to be a positive influence. Watch for ways to
  encourage fellowship, peace, and joy in the church family.
- Demonstrate faithfulness. This is not a time to
  relinquish responsibilities or slack off in church ministry.
  Faithfulness is to God, not to the former pastor.
- Fill vacuums. If the former pastor's wife served in the
  life of your church, consider ways you can help fill those
  voids temporarily. Example: she may have taught a class or
  visited homebound.
- Realize that your husband's responsibilities as a deacon
  may be greater during these months, and pray for him.
- If the pastor will live in a parsonage, deacon wives could
  be divided into teams to aggressively update the house.
  Make every attempt to provide a home for your pastor
  that is nicer than your own! Does it need cleaning,
  repairs, paint, or carpet? What can be done to enhance the
  exterior?
- Perk up the pastor's office. Offer your assistance to
  update, clean or paint to provide a professional, appealing
  office space for God's chosen leader for your church.
  Provide spacious bookshelves and up-to-date equipment.
- Take a fresh look at church facilities. If buildings have
  become cluttered and dingy, plan work days for deacon
  wives and friends to clean. An unkempt or outdated
  church facility does not reflect a great love for God and
  will not help to welcome a new leader.

When the new pastor arrives

- Enthusiastically welcome the pastor God has provided. Organize a welcome gift from the deacons and wives, such as a beautiful plant or flowers for the pastor's office and home.
- Repeat your name each time you encounter the new pastor and wife for the first few months. They have many people to learn and will appreciate your thoughtfulness.
- Pray for the pastor's wife as she transitions. Send her a monthly encouragement note. Tell her that you are committed to help and encourage her. Give her your phone and e-mail so she can call if she gets lost, has a flat tire, or needs to hear a friendly voice. Ascertain that she knows you are available to help her with ministry projects or other needs.
- Deacon wives could be divided into teams to help with preparations to receive the pastor and family, assisting as needed with receptions, welcome packets, or other arrangements.
- If the pastor purchases a home, ask permission to plan a workday before they move there. Clean windows perfectly, line shelves, make small repairs, mow the lawn, etc.
- If the pastor has children, help with school info, phone numbers, and names of children their age, babysitter names, and information about city activities. Stock their pantry with snacks. A welcome gift can impact children's enthusiasm. Our new pastorate in Dallas gave our children personalized Dallas Cowboy jerseys and cowboy hats.
- On a city map, mark the church location along with parks, sites of interest, schools, etc.

- Prepare a fun "glad you're here" booklet from the deacon wives. Include a city map with deacon wives' homes and favorite restaurants marked.
- After she has had a couple of weeks to unpack, invite the pastor's wife to lunch or coffee.

These suggestions can be applied to any church staff position. If your church has support staff, such a minister of music or youth, they need your encouragement as well. Befriend them and love them as you love your senior pastor.

A deacon's wife can make a difference! Get ready to love and serve alongside a new minister and his wife. Read these words aloud: "Anyone who welcomes a prophet because he is a prophet will receive a prophet's reward. And anyone who welcomes a righteous person because he's righteous will receive a righteous person's reward" (Matt. 10:41).

MARITAL PROBLEMS

Don't just watch helplessly as marriages erode or explode right there in your beloved church family. God is the author of that marriage. Perhaps He can use you, a deacon wife, to help in this dreaded situation. Need a few starter suggestions?

Duo ministry. Ministry *to* a couple in marital trouble can be done *by* a couple. Invite them for coffee. Laugh together, listen carefully, and pray for them aloud. Ask how you can help. Be there for them. Sit near them at church. Communicate often. Help the couple develop friendships with other Christian couples.

Girl talk. If she chooses to talk with you, dear deacon wife, listen carefully. Pray silently while she speaks. Never take sides or pry. You don't need to know the details. God is certainly big enough to mend the marriage, so pray for the couple. Your listening ministry should be exclusively to the wife, not the husband. With the exception of your pastor, don't tell another person about their problems. Not a word! (Your reputation is at stake here.)

Unless you are a counselor with a degree, leave counseling to your pastor. If your pastor is not aware of the problem, ask if she and her husband will talk with him or if she would prefer that you inform him. I'm amazed at how often God uses a consultation with the pastor to heal marital problems. Most pastors will refer extended marriage counseling to a Christian professional.

Tangible ministry. Purchase a Christian book or CD on marriage. Help arrange a babysitter for an evening. Offer a friend's lake cottage for a getaway weekend. Help them find a Christ-centered marriage retreat.

Would you invest twelve dollars in stamps and two and a half hours of your time to help that marriage? Tell her that you are committed to pray *every day* this month for God's healing in their marriage. Purchase thirty stamps and mail a daily note to her— Scripture, prayer, quote, encouragement, or compliment. Spend five minutes each day on your knees, praying to the God of the universe on their behalf. You may continue on a weekly or monthly basis after that. God's listening.

Bonus idea. If families are assigned to deacons at your church, celebrate marriage. Take each married couple for lunch, snap a flattering photo of them, and present the framed photo as a gift. Dennis and Vicki Barton are the deacon and deacon wife assigned to Steve and me at our church. On our wedding anniversary every year, they mail us a card with a written prayer for our marriage. What an encouragement!

Bottom line. Don't just look the other way when marital strife hits the church. Deacons and their wives can help encourage joyful marriages and can surround troubled marriages with God's love.

Practical Ways to Help a Woman in Marital Trouble

1. Listen carefully.
2. Pray while she speaks.
3. Don't take sides.
4. Speak to her at church.
5. Give her a Christian book or CD on marriage. Ask your pastor for a recommendation.
6. Arrange a babysitter for an evening out.
7. Help them find a Christian marriage retreat.
8. Help them pay to attend it.
9. Offer a friend's lake cottage for a getaway weekend.
10. Invest in thirty postage stamps. Pray for her every day this month; then mail a note with a Scripture.
11. Ask them to go on a double date with you and your husband. Laugh. Listen. Pray aloud for their marriage.
12. Sit with them at church.
13. Communicate often. Help them find other couple friends in the church.
14. Refer them to pastoral counseling or other Christian counselor.
15. Pray. Pray. Pray.

MENTORING

Titus 2 mandates women to teach the younger women. As a pastor's wife, I've observed wonderful models of deacon wives mentoring younger women in the church. Some mentor women they met at a church function or women with problems or women who are new Christians. Others mentor new or potential deacon wives. Will you take the Titus 2 challenge?

Allow me to share a few simple mentoring tips.

1.   Ask God to direct you to a woman to mentor. Pay attention to younger women at church. The influence of older Christian women has made an enormous impact on my life, and I have enjoyed mentoring several younger women over the years. No matter your age, there is some younger woman in your church who would benefit from your life experience and godly wisdom.

2.   A mentoring relationship may be informal, but most often it is stated. For example, my adult daughter intentionally mentors several younger women. She and each younger woman determine together that they want to establish a mentoring-type relationship and make a plan to meet weekly for instruction, encouragement, and accountability.

3.   Be flexible but diligent. Schedule a time to meet one-on-one each week. Mentoring becomes a part of your lifestyle. Select a time convenient for both ladies. Meet Tuesday mornings at the doughnut shop, Thursday afternoons in your living room, or Sundays before Bible class. During a crisis or vacation, stay consistent by using phone or e-mail.

4.   What will we talk about? Titus 2:3–5 instructs the older woman "to teach what is good, so that they may encourage the young women to love their husbands and children, to be sensible, pure, good homemakers, and submissive to their husbands, so that God's message will not be slandered." Notice the two verbs: *teach* and *encourage*. Make a checklist of these seven topics and refer to it. Remember, the purpose is spiritual. You are to encourage the younger woman to be

a Christian mother, a Christian wife, a Christian woman.

5.   Methods may vary. Do a Bible study together. Spend time chatting about how God is working in your lives. Discuss a Christian book you're both reading. Spend time praying together. My friend Carolyn mentors by meeting for weekly church outreach. As they make visits, she models personal witnessing and uses drive time for sharing and accountability. Cindy mentors over coffee. They meet at the coffee shop or take a coffee thermos to the city park.

6.   Accountability happens. Every week, ask hard questions. How is God working in your life? Are you being the wife, the mother, the woman that God desires? Have you been faithful this week in reading God's Word and spending time with Him? How can I pray for you?

7.   In the beginning share your life story and hear her story. Talk about how you met Christ and His impact on your lives today. Hear her heart.

8.   Be approachable. She must be able to discuss tough questions with you, with the assurance of your prayers, help, confidentiality and encouragement.

9.   Help her discover her spiritual gifts and joyfully use them in God's church. Carefully observe her interests and strengths. Include her in ministry with you when possible.

10. Personalize mentoring. Learn her children's names, her favorite color, and her hobbies. Acknowledge her birthday. Take her to lunch. Recommend good books. Invite her to your home. Speak well of her. Be her best cheerleader. Compliment her. Introduce her to your friends at church. Laugh together.

11. Love her anyway. She isn't perfect. Neither are you. Don't expect her to act just like you or dress just like you or minister like you. God created her as His unique child.

12. Vigilantly set an example in every area of life. Titus 2:3 says, "Older women are to be reverent in behavior, not slanderers, not addicted to much wine." She'll observe your attitudes, priorities, and body language. She'll watch how you worship, how you dress with modesty, how you interact with your husband. She'll notice how you spend your money, your time, and your energies. Discretion is imperative. Read Proverbs 11:22, and remember the pig.

13. Never gossip with her. Never gossip about her. Dozens of Scripture verses condemn gossip. Carefully set an example in your speech.

14. As you study God's Word, watch for verses to encourage her. Write the Scripture on a note card and share it with her.

15. Pray for her daily. Pray aloud with her. Demonstrate dependence on our great God, and celebrate when He answers prayer.

No matter your age, dear deacon's wife, there is a younger woman in your church who could learn from your Christian life experience. Take it seriously, and mentor well. Will you pray today about mentoring a younger woman?

MINISTRY: IT'S ALL ABOUT HIM

Your acts of ministry are not Girl Scout good deeds or a campaign to improve your reputation. Acts of Christian ministry must be done in Jesus' name. Before you leave a ministry visit, share a comforting Scripture and voice a brief prayer to God. Assure her that others in your church will pray for her. Remind her that God cares. You represent not only your church and your pastor but also your God! You are the "aroma of Christ" (2 Cor. 2:15 NIV).

Tips for Deacon Wives

Here's a fun checklist of some ideas for a deacon wife. Select one you'd enjoy and do it this week.

❏ Mail one encouragement note to a church member every day.

❏ Show up when it counts.

❏ Print personal business cards.

❏ Love your husband.

❏ Keep a calendar. Jot birthdays, death anniversaries, and reminders of needs.

❏ Carry a small New Testament in your purse. Always be ready to share Jesus.

❏ Find at least one ministry within the church and give it your very best.

❏ Prepare a list of favorite ministry Scriptures to keep in your Bible.

❏ Plant a rosebush or zinnias. Watch for ways to use them in ministry.

❏ When you see a guest in worship, sit near her.

❏ Get involved in your community in some way. Share Jesus with the lost.

❏ Freeze soup or casseroles for future ministry needs.

❏ Go on a mission trip. It will change you forever.

❏ Begin a notebook of new members, new Christians, marriages, funerals.

- ❏ Faithfully, joyfully use your spiritual gifts within the church.
- ❏ Help in Sunday school or small groups in some way. Do it well.
- ❏ Stop by the nursery occasionally and offer a compliment to those workers.
- ❏ Love your pastor and staff members and their families.
- ❏ Pay special attention to custodial workers or volunteers in the church office.
- ❏ Get off the pedestal. Be an example of a servant leader.
- ❏ Never speak a negative word in your church or about your church.
- ❏ Take notes in a sermon journal.
- ❏ Lavishly love your children without worshipping them.
- ❏ Respect your husband.
- ❏ Ask your deacon husband to pray for you before you go to work or to sleep.
- ❏ Never complain about God's work or the church to your children.
- ❏ See every church member as God does. Love them.
- ❏ Smile. It means a lot.
- ❏ Keep on growing. Participate in a Bible study. Read Christian books.
- ❏ Practice hospitality. Keep practicing.
- ❏ Carry a church directory in the car. Keep one by the telephone. Learn names.
- ❏ Be assertive in looking for new faces at church. Make a connection.
- ❏ Always carry your favorite witnessing tract.

❑ Take your pastor's wife to lunch once each month. Put it on your calendar.

❑ When there's a death, make a phone call right away. Pray on the phone.

❑ Joyfully give more than a tithe.

❑ Act like it's a privilege to serve God's people. It is.

❑ Read God's Word every day.

❑ Make a personal goal to share Jesus with someone at least once a month.

❑ Always be cultivating a witnessing relationship with someone new.

❑ Participate in church activities and ministries.

❑ Don't be in charge of everything at church. Help others find a ministry.

❑ Ask your husband how you can help him.

❑ Never threaten to leave the church. (Never threaten divorce either!)

❑ Never serve "roast preacher" for Sunday lunch.

❑ Do something good anonymously.

❑ Never retaliate. God can handle it.

❑ Show up for church outreach.

❑ Watch for ways you can help during worship services.

❑ Attempt to be in your place of ministry at your church every Sunday.

❑ Try to know as much as possible about your church.

❑ Teach your kids to love the church.

❑ Never ask your husband about confidential church business.

❑ Don't rest on "I used to's." God has a job for you today.

- ❑ Ask for a list of last week's church guests. Call and welcome them.
- ❑ Learn from your pastor's wife.
- ❑ Be available to help with women who make decisions for Christ in worship.
- ❑ Be ready to help in times of crisis, in both your church and community.
- ❑ Find a way to use your hobby for ministry in Jesus' name.
- ❑ Buy a few brightly colored pillowcases. Buy cards in bulk.
- ❑ Pick up an extra church bulletin to deliver to a hospitalized or shut-in friend.
- ❑ Deliver a cupcake with a lit candle on a homebound member's birthday.
- ❑ Remember the pig (Prov. 11:22).
- ❑ Show self-control in hard areas of life (chocolate, shopping, temper, etc.).
- ❑ Set a great example for younger women in every area of life.
- ❑ Honor God by being the best employee at your work.
- ❑ Begin a Bible study with your neighbors or coworkers.
- ❑ Never disguise gossip as a prayer request.
- ❑ Occasionally invite a guest at church to join you for lunch.
- ❑ Pray while you dress for church every Sunday.
- ❑ Pray aloud on the phone with someone in crisis.
- ❑ Honor God in unspoken ways, i.e., body language, dress, parenting.
- ❑ Keep a list of elderly widows in your purse; visit when you have a moment.

❏ Buy thirty stamps; mail a prayer note daily for a month to a member in crisis.

❏ Tell your pastor's wife that she can call on you anytime she needs someone to help with ministry or a church need. Then rise to her request.

❏ Learn the names of children and teens at church.

❏ Mentor a younger Christian woman (Titus 2:3–5).

❏ Invite another deacon's wife to go with you for hospital/ministry visits. Stop for coffee afterward.

⇥ 6 ⇤

Worth the Effort

D on't become "weary in well doing" (Gal. 6:9 KJV). It's worth your effort to minister in God's name, so keep on shining!

Worth Your Effort to Serve

> We must do the works of Him who sent Me while it is day. Night is coming when no one can work. (John 9:4)

Whatever you do in serving Christ will result in eternal rewards. As you survey your response to the "My Ministry at My Church" form on pages 136–138, please notice two points:

1. The need for volunteers in your local church is vast and imperative. This list is only a fraction of opportunities to serve in your church.
2. Allow others to help. Don't quit doing a ministry to which God has called you. But if you are overworked, begin today to train up an assistant who can carry on that task. Pay special attention to help women in your church find a place of joyful ministry. If you do it all, you steal their joy!

A popular topic for women today is learning to say "no." May I challenge you, instead, to learn to say yes? Too many of us say yes to a myriad of trivial jobs that won't matter in eternity and say no to ministries where God has called us. There are Christian women who spend hours every week volunteering for worthy secular organizations or parachurch groups while their church is void of necessary workers. Yes, you should be involved in your community, but the church must be top priority. Christ died for the church. The church is God's bride. She deserves our best efforts.

Before you respond to a need in the church, ask God for wisdom. He could prompt you to say, "Yes, I would love to do that." Or, "No, God hasn't released me to take that responsibility, but I think I know a woman in our church who may be interested in helping do that."

Steve and I were standing in a reception line, meeting all the deacons and deacon wives at the church where Steve would be the new pastor. As several dozen of them came through the line, we asked each one, "How do you serve here at the church?" Later in our hotel room we lamented together about a consistent response we'd heard: "Well, I used to . . ."

Don't rest on "what I used to do." God has work for you to do today. Oh, I know, contemporary thought says that you should learn to say no and put yourself first and let someone else do it. But Jesus taught that whoever wants to become great must become a servant (Matt. 20:26). Many women today, even deacon wives, are so adept at saying no that they're almost good for nothing! Ask God to show you opportunities to serve Him. Keep your eyes and your heart open, seek His wisdom, and say yes every time you can!

Discover your spiritual gifts and use them. If you and your husband are busy about ministering in His church, it will function better, harmony will be enhanced, and the church will grow.

When you serve God, give your best, 100-percent effort. Don't settle for mediocrity. God deserves our wholehearted devotion and service. Faithfully serve Him as if it's a top priority and high privilege. It is! After all, you're serving the Creator of the universe and the Savior of your soul. Ask yourself, do I give more effort to the PTA, scout troop, or community club than to my Father's house?

When you serve, serve joyfully. There are hundreds of Scriptures about joy. In Deuteronomy 28:47, God punished the Israelites because they did not serve Him "with joy and a cheerful heart." There is great pleasure in serving our great God. Never serve Him grudgingly. Serve God with great gladness. And smile when you serve.

> Based on the gift they have received, everyone should use it to serve others, as good managers of the varied grace of God. (1 Pet. 4:10)

What Is Your Spiritual Gift?

Take this online exam:

www.lifeway.com/lwc/files/lwcF_MYCS_030526_Spiritual_Gifts_Survey.pdf

My spiritual gift(s) is (are):

_____

An Attitude of Servitude
Test

- If strangers were watching me at church, would they catch me serving?
- When I notice something needing attention at church, do I complain about it or help to solve it?
- Do I intentionally seek ways to help my pastor's wife in ministry? Does my church staff know they can call on me to help with ministry needs?
- When a need arises at church, do I try to get by with the bare minimum, or do I truly serve "as unto the Lord" (Eph. 5:22 KJV)?
- Am I constantly aware of needs around me at church? Do I do something about them?
- Do others know that I enjoy serving God? Does it show on my face?

What If . . . ?

Take this quick test.

You're in line for a dinner at the church. You notice that the line hardly moves, and they're obviously shorthanded in the food line. What do you do?

❑ Complain loudly that someone should have organized this better.

❑ Grab an apron and joyfully offer to help serve.

❑ Cut in line.

You're walking down the hallway at church and notice a woman who appears to be lost. What do you do?

❑ Walk on by. No one likes nosy people.

❑ Smile and say a silent prayer. You mustn't be late for your class.

❑ Ask if you can help her and then walk with her to her destination.

The couple in front of you in the grocery checkout line mentions that they just moved to town. You kindly . . .

❑ Turn away. Your mom taught you not to talk to strangers, after all.

❑ Explain local politics and give directions to the nearest Starbucks.

❑ Invite them to worship at your church Sunday and arrange to meet them at the front door.

You just learned of the death of a church member. What do you do?

❑ Notify the church office.

- ❏ Call and pray with the widow on the phone.
- ❏ Go to the home to comfort his widow.
- ❏ Help with the children.
- ❏ Organize food for the family.
- ❏ Ask what you can do to help (phone calls, airport runs, cleaning).
- ❏ All of the above and anything else God prompts.

You just learned of a community crisis that will affect your whole town. You immediately . . .

- ❏ Call your church staff to offer to help plan or work.
- ❏ Pray and ask God how you can serve Him in this situation.
- ❏ Check on church members who may have a need.
- ❏ All of the above.

My Ministry at My Church

Please complete this form, listing ways you currently minister in your church. Write additional hands-on ministries in the margins.

> "I am able to do all things through Him who strengthens me" (Phil. 4:13).

WEEKLY/REGULARLY

- ❏ Prison ministry
- ❏ Church greeter
- ❏ Church library
- ❏ Hospital visits
- ❏ Drama team
- ❏ Choir or praise team
- ❏ Minister to bereaved
- ❏ Faithful attender
- ❏ Handyman projects
- ❏ Drive church van
- ❏ Apartment ministry
- ❏ Minister to widows
- ❏ Disciple a new believer
- ❏ Teach/assist with choirs
- ❏ Church mission trip
- ❏ Benevolence projects
- ❏ Lead someone to Christ
- ❏ Teach/assist discipleship class
- ❏ Sunday school/small-group teacher
- ❏ Sunday school department director
- ❏ Teach preschoolers during church activities
- ❏ Coach church sports teams as a ministry
- ❏ Help with counseling during worship invitations
- ❏ Sunday school secretary, outreach, group leader

HANDS-ON MINISTRY

- ❏ Plan Sunday school or church fellowships
- ❏ Vacation Bible school teacher or director
- ❏ Assist with baptismal or Lord's Supper prep
- ❏ Phone or notes to sick, bereaved, or homebound
- ❏ Write encouragement notes to ministry staff
- ❏ Help organize, prepare, or serve funeral dinners
- ❏ Help serve or prepare Wednesday night dinner
- ❏ Assist with new member welcome
- ❏ Serve on a committee:

  _____

- ❏ Chaperone youth/children's events
- ❏ Lead in a project to help a missionary
- ❏ Take a prayer hour in church prayer chapel
- ❏ Use my home for church events
- ❏ Pray for ministers, missionaries, leaders, members

WEEKLY/REGULARLY

- ❏ Teach/assist missions groups
- ❏ Invite someone to church
- ❏ Visit town newcomers
- ❏ Visit sick in their homes
- ❏ Church office volunteer
- ❏ Church benevolence
- ❏ Leader in women's ministry
- ❏ Help with setup for events
- ❏ Host baby/wedding showers
- ❏ Sound/tech team

HANDS-ON MINISTRY

- ❏ Orchestra, praise band
- ❏ Homebound/nursing homes
- ❏ Outreach calls or visits
- ❏ Help begin church plant
- ❏ Mentor younger woman
- ❏ Sponsor child for camp
- ❏ Decor, bulletin boards
- ❏ Special events, i.e., fall festival

Worth Your Effort to Pray
(taken from *Deacon* Magazine)

You have an important appointment—a meeting with the Creator of the universe. He's waiting to talk to you. It's called "prayer." There are thousands of practical, effective ways a deacon wife can impact the ministry of her church. But this is the big one . . . pray.

Prayer is your secret weapon, dear Deacon Wife. The battles of life and ministry can become overwhelming if you fail to utilize prayer. Why should a deacon's wife pray?

- It's not an option. We are commanded to pray.
- We're weak, but great power is available through prayer.
- Prayer protects. Know your weaknesses. Commit those areas of life to Him.
- You're not omnipresent. God is. Through prayer, you invite God into the lives of those for whom you pray 24/7 —not just when you're with them.
- Prayer changes things. Whatever the need, our great God can handle it.

A deacon's wife and I sat in the driveway, terrified at the enormity of our task. A man in our church had committed suicide just a few minutes earlier, and we were there to comfort his wife. No, there were no words that could bring him back, but we had a great and powerful resource: prayer. Before we walked to the door, we sat in the car and prayed together. We begged our Father to give us wisdom and strength. We asked that He would give us His peace, and help us to minister to her in His name. We prayed for the grieving widow inside the house, and asked her Creator to cradle her and comfort her. When we rang the doorbell, she answered quickly, grabbed us both in a bear hug, and said "I saw you in the car praying for me. That's exactly what I needed."

> Now this is the confidence we have before Him: whenever we ask anything according to His will, He hears us. And if we know that He hears whatever we ask, we know that we have what we have asked Him for. (1 John 5:14–15)

Some Practical Prayer Tips for a Deacon Wife

Stop, drop, and pray. A church member stops you in the ladies room to share a need or concern. Stop right there, drop what you're doing, take her hand, and offer a prayer on her behalf. Prayer changes things. God's listening!

Pray during church. Have you ever seen someone check her watch during worship? That won't happen to you if you are busy praying. Pray silently during the service for the guests, the sermon, child-care workers, ushers, even the announcements.

Pray before you speak. Whether it's to teach a children's Bible lesson or to talk with your best friend on the phone, say a prayer before you speak. Why? Because "out of the overflow of the heart the mouth speaks" (Matt. 12:34 NIV).

Get caught praying. Teach your children to pray. Pray with them for specific requests. Prayer walk at the church building with them on Saturday morning. Allow your children to see you and hear you pray.

Pray on the phone. When someone calls about a need or problem, voice a prayer before you hang up. Pray aloud, right there on the phone.

Pray during deacons meetings. Why not begin a new practice of praying when your husband attends a deacons meeting at church? While your husband meets with the pastor and deacons, you have a meeting with God. Pray for wisdom and discernment for the deacons and staff. God's listening.

Remember what you prayed. Have you ever kept a prayer journal? It's an ongoing list of prayer requests you have brought to the Father. Add requests each day to your journal, highlighting answered prayers. Your journal will soon be full of yellow! Steve and I had wanted to have a baby for seven long years before God blessed us with our first son. Years later I found my old prayer journal. Precisely *nine months* before our son's birth, I'd written a petition to God, asking Him to bless us with children. And we had three in a row! Oh, I already knew those children were from God, but my written journal and its precise timing reminded me that God was actively listening.

Pray for your favorite deacon. Your deacon husband needs your prayer support. Pray for God's wisdom and strength as he serves as a deacon. Remind him of your prayers.

Say it. Pray faithfully for church staff, deacons, teachers, and other leaders. Tell them you're praying. Send a note to remind them of your prayers.

Pray by name. Use a church directory to pray for church members from A to Z. Check off names with a colored pen. When you've prayed for the entire list, get a different color pen and begin again.

Pray when you minister. Delivering a casserole? Say a silent prayer before you ring their doorbell. When you make an outreach contact or visit the homebound, hospitalized, or bereaved, voice a prayer for them before you leave.

Pray on your way. I know! I know! You're a busy woman with family, work, church, chores, and ministry. Some days you may feel there is no time left to talk with God. How can you possibly find time to pray? During everyday moments of life, talk with God. Look for minutes when you are exercising, shopping, driving, waiting, or walking.

Shower power. My daughter, who works with youth in her church, has a unique prayer plan. She made a list of her youth and youth workers, put it inside a plastic report cover, and taped it on the wall in her shower. Every day she prays for each of them. Tape your list by your makeup mirror, ironing board, or computer screen.

Sunday prep prayer. Begin a new habit. While you're dressing for church each Sunday, pray. Pray for the pastor and leaders as they prepare. Pray for church members. Think about each thing that will occur in God's house today and pray. A deacon wife in our church brought her children to the church building every Saturday morning for a few minutes. They walked past each classroom and pew, praying aloud for the people God would touch there on Sunday.

Celebrate answered prayer. When God answers a specific prayer for a member of your church, invite her for coffee or lunch to celebrate!

Dear deacon wife, you *must* spend time in prayer. Women in your church are watching how you respond to life events. Respond with prayer.

Deacon wives are instructed to be faithful in everything (1 Tim. 3:11). Be faithful in prayer. A deacon wife can impact ministry in her church in thousands of ways. Prayer is the biggest one.

> Pray constantly. (1 Thess. 5:17)

> If My people who are called by My name humble themselves, pray and seek My face, . . . then I will hear from heaven, forgive their sin, and heal their land. (2 Chron. 7:14)

Final Exam

"Wives, too, must be _____
_____
_____
_____
_____."

Bonus: Where is this verse found in the Bible?
_____

A Note from the Author

Dearest Deacon Wife,

I hope you've enjoyed our chat about deacon wives. You're in for the most exciting days of your life! I'm praying that God will use you in an amazing way in your local church as you work hand in hand with your deacon husband.

I'd love to hear how God is working through deacon wives in your church. E-mail your stories anytime!

For lots more ministry ideas, I hope you'll check out my books, *Fresh Ideas—1,000 Ways to Grow a Thriving and Energetic Church* (B&H Publishing Group, 2007) and *Fresh Ideas for Women's Ministry* (B&H Publishing Group, 2008) as well as my "She Said" column for deacon wives in *Deacon* magazine.

And don't forget, love Him. Love Him.

Diana
www.keeponshining.com

APPENDIX

Teaching Plan

Purpose: This book may be taught as a six-week class to encourage, educate, and motivate new and current deacon wives. It may also be used as a personal study for a deacon wife.

Who Attends? The class should be limited to women who are married to active deacons in your church. If the church has selected new deacons, those wives should be included.

Special Guests

Session 1. Pastor's wife, first ten minutes of class.

Session 2. Pastor's wife and other paid ministry staff members' wives and female ministry staff members attend last ten minutes of class.

Session 5. Pastor's wife and any other pastoral ministry staff wives or female ministry staff members attend last fifteen minutes of class.

Session 6. Pastor and pastor's wife are invited for opening reception. Pastor's wife stays for entire class, if available, and makes ending presentation.

Schedule: Six one-hour meetings, planned at a time convenient for attenders. If preferred, the class could be done as a retreat, with six one-hour classes interspersed with fellowship activities.

Invitation: Each deacon wife in your church should receive a verbal *and* written invitation at least one month before the study begins. One week before class begins, the deacon chairman's wife may call to remind each deacon wife. The printed invitation may be:

- An attractive printed invitation, either hand delivered or mailed.
- Deliver one fresh flower, tied with a ribbon to this invitation:

Fresh Ideas for Hope Baptist Deacon Wives Only
Six-week study based on a new book,
Deacon Wives by Diana Davis
Begins Sunday, September 5 at 6 p.m.
Church Parlor

- A 26-ounce round box of salt, with an attractive invitation attached:

Shake! Shake! Shake!
You are the salt of the earth.
Please join us for a six-week class for
Calvary Baptist Church Deacon Wives
beginning Sunday, September 5
6 p.m. in Room 254

Makeup Class: If a deacon wife must be absent from a class, the deacon chairman's wife can arrange a time to discuss the class session with her. Provide an audiotape or CD of the teaching portion of the class for her to review.

Classroom: Reserve the most attractive classroom at the church. Fresh flowers would be a nice touch for the sign-in table, and chairs will be rearranged weekly.

Teacher: Class may be led by the deacon chairman's wife, the pastor's wife, or another female leader invited by the pastor and deacon chairman. If the deacon chairman's wife is not teaching, she will assist with preparations and act as hostess. She will begin weekly classes on time, open with prayer, and introduce the teacher.

Note: If the pastor's wife is teaching the class, a different person should lead the discussion in session 2 on encouraging the pastor and pastor's wife.

Materials

A copy of *Deacon Wives* book for each attender.

Timer, index cards, pens, whiteboard, chalkboard, PowerPoint projection (optional).

Weekly visuals as noted below.

Preparations

The deacon chairman's wife will take the lead on preparations. It would be desirable for her to share (delegate) these assignments with several other deacon wives.

1. Prepare and distribute printed invitations to each deacon wife, one month before class.

2. Order a copy of *Deacon Wives* book for each deacon wife. Personally distribute them one week before class begins.

3. Make a personal telephone reminder to each deacon wife one week before class begins. This should be done by the deacon chairman's wife, if possible.

4. Photo project. Snap a quick digital picture of each participant as they arrive for the first class. Create a simple

directory or photo page with deacon wife's name, husband's name, and contact information, including e-mail address. Distribute these in session 3. Even better, add photos of pastoral staff wives.

5. Name tags. Print names in a font large enough to read from six feet away. Consider using plastic name tags, collecting them at the end of each class. On the back of four name tags, place one of the following symbols: ★, ☺, ♥, ✿

6. Greeters. One or two deacon wives may be recruited to arrive early to staff a registration table and welcome attenders each session.

7. Homework e-mail. Send a brief e-mail weekly with a review of assignments.

8. Session 6 snacks. Prepare drinks and snacks. Use decorative napkins and a centerpiece of flowers (for presentation ceremony).

You may use downloadable PowerPoint presentations each week, if desired. A few minutes of preparation will be necessary to personalize it for your church.

Session 1: Hello, Mrs. Deacon

Class setup: Chairs are placed in two long rows approximately two feet apart, facing one another. Since you know the expected attendance, set up the exact number of chairs. A single chair or podium is placed at the end for the leader. An index card and pen are on each seat.

Preparation

__ Make copies: Job Interview form; homework assignment.

__ Invite the pastor's wife to do the welcome for this first session.

__ Recruit a Scripture reader ahead of time (see job application section).

__ Recruit artist for "Perfect Deacon's Wife" visual. Hang large paper.

__ Carefully research the answers for the "know-it-all" activity, using www.namb.net, www.imb.org, and your church office. Prepare a whiteboard, PowerPoint, or poster of the Know-It-All chart (below), and hide the third-column answers with a cloth.

Arrival: As each deacon wife arrives, take a quick photo of her and give her a name tag prepared in advance.

Welcome: Deacon chairman's wife begins class on time, welcoming deacon wives and introducing the pastor's wife.

Opening Comment and Prayer: Pastor's wife gives a greeting to deacon wives and voices the opening prayer. (Pastor's wife may want to stay for introductions.)

Twelve-Word Introductions

Ladies are given a few minutes to chat with the women sitting across from them to get to know each other. Let them know that after three minutes, they will be asked to introduce the person facing them. Here's the catch: they can only use twelve words. Encourage them to use index cards for notes and then begin twelve-word introductions. If your group is large, several rows of two chairs may work and report separately. (Pastor's wife may leave after this activity.)

Introductory Activity: "The Perfect Deacon Wife"

Recruit the most artistic (or brave) deacon wife ahead of time. Mount three adjacent poster boards or a large white paper on the wall. The artist uses markers to sketch the outline of a woman before class. A stick figure will work fine. Tell the class that our artist has three minutes to create the perfect deacon wife. Class members will coach her by calling out characteristics or expectations that church members may have of the perfect deacon wife. As class members call out instructions, the artist quickly adds words and props to the figure. She adds every suggestion, whether it's right or wrong, silly or serious. Make this fast and fun.

Job Application

Distribute job application forms from page 11 and ask each woman to complete them.

After forms are complete, ask women to turn to 1 Timothy 3:8–13 in their Bibles to discover the biblical expectations for a deacon wife. As the prearranged reader reads the verses clearly, ask women to raise their hands when verse 11 is read. Invite women to memorize this verse during the next six weeks and to try to live up to its challenge for deacon wives. Use a wide black marker to write "1 Timothy 3:11" across the "perfect deacon wife" art.

Ambassador Lessons

Oral Pop Quiz. Women in the left row of chairs are asked to stand quietly and move one chair to the left, creating new partners for this assignment. The taller of the two has thirty seconds to answer the oral test question to her partner. Read the question aloud:

> You meet an acquaintance in the local bookstore, and she asks, "What's going on at your church these days?" How will you respond? You have thirty seconds to answer. Go!

All women respond to their partners at the same time. At the end of thirty seconds, call time. Read the question once again and allow the other partner to respond. Remind deacon wives that they are ambassadors for their Lord and their church and must always be ready to tell someone about what God is doing in His church.

"Know-It-All" Activity. Talk about the importance of knowing facts about the church. Ask the deacon wife with a ✿ on the back of her name tag to write answers on the chart as ladies attempt to guess the correct answers to twelve questions on the visual. (The correct answers in the third column are covered with a cloth.) After you've written all their guesses in the first column, unveil the correct answers. This will be a lighthearted way to encourage women to be informed about their church. Challenge deacon wives to read their church newsletter and pay attention to church announcements so they will be well-informed and ready to tell others about their church.

Our Church	Our Guesses	Actual Number
Number of people baptized during past twelve months		
Number church members		
Average Sunday school attendance		
Number new members last year		
Number missionaries in North America supported by our church through Cooperative Program and Annie Armstrong offering		Appx 5,000 (North American Mission Board, www. namb.net)
Number overseas missionaries supported by our church through Cooperative Program and Lottie Moon offering		Appx 5,184 (See International Mission Board, www. imb.org)
Number first-time guests at our church in past two months		
Which is fastest growing Sunday school class this year?		
Money given to Cooperative Program for missionaries		
Number members in nursing homes and homebound		

Attendance at (largest outreach last year, i.e., Easter pageant or vacation Bible school)		
Add one more impressive number here, such as number of new babies, number new Sunday school classes, or number at youth camp		

Something Good (optional activity). Ask women in left row to move one seat to the left once again to establish new conversation partners. Discuss the statement on the whiteboard:

"Talk about some good things that are going on in our church right now."

After the groups have talked for a minute together, add this question to the board and ask them to respond: "What are you doing to encourage it?"

Prayer Partners: Ask ladies in the left-hand row to stand and move down one chair to their left. The person across from them will be their assigned prayer partner for a week. Invite them to exchange phone numbers before they leave and to meet for coffee or chat by phone sometime during the coming week.

Homework: Distribute printed homework assignments for next week's class. Dismiss on time with prayer.

Homework Assignment for Session 2

__ Review the eight tips from today's lesson in the book. Choose one where you will try to improve and report your results next week.

__ Read through chapter 2 of *Deacon Wives* book.

__ Meet your prayer partner for coffee, if possible, or chat by phone. Share about your salvation and your life journey as a Christian.

__ Review 1 Timothy 3:11.

__ During the next six weeks, attempt to make at least one hospital or sick visit and one homebound or nursing home visit. Take another deacon wife or staff wife with you.

Session 2: Encouragement

Preparation

1. Attach a small magnet to the back of each deacon wife photo taken last week. Hang photos in groups of two on one wall. (These will be new prayer partner assignments.)
2. Print copies of homework assignments and Pop Test in chapter 2. Make a sign: "Please be seated near your prayer partner from last week. Thanks!"
3. Photo page or directory of deacon wives will be distributed during Session 3; finalize its data.
4. Invite pastor's wife (and other ministry staff wives or female ministry staff members) to attend the last twenty minutes of Session 2.
5. Recruit an additional person (not a deacon wife) to arrive twenty minutes before class ending to take a digital group photo with pastor's wife.
6. Ask each deacon officer's wife to participate in the closing prayer.
7. Bring a basket or silver tray and an assortment of Golden Delicious apples, enough for each deacon wife.

Room Setup: Arrange the chairs in a large V shape. The leader will sit at the center chair facing the group. (Later in class, the pastor's wife will take that seat.) Place the pop test under each chair.

Arrive: Write one line of "I will respect my husband" on the chalkboard or whiteboard. As each woman arrives, invite her to continue writing the phrase until the next person arrives. That next person continues writing until the next arrives, and so forth. This is just for fun, but we'll address the topic seriously in this class.

Welcome: The deacon chairman's wife begins exactly on time to welcome the group and lead in prayer. Tell the women that the pastor's wife will arrive later and ask if each of them will plan to say a word of compliment or encouragement to her. Give each deacon wife an apple to present to the pastor's wife when they encourage her.

Mixer: "I-Game": Read the following list, asking women to stand if it applies to them, and then be seated as you keep reading. (Feel free to add a few!)

I jog.
I ski.
I fish.
I cook.
I quilt.
I garden.
I scrapbook.
I love flying.
I clip coupons.
I love to laugh.
I'm good at Sudoku.
I work a part-time job.
I'm employed full-time.
I have teenage children.
I change diapers every day.
I enjoy making hospital visits.
I know the capital of Uruguay.
I teach a Sunday school class.
I attended worship last Sunday.

I welcomed a guest last Sunday.

I drive downtown at least weekly.

I wrote a kind note to the pastor's wife this week.

I collect wind chimes (substitute something you know someone collects).

On these last four, don't stand. Just think about your answer.

During this past week, I was worthy of respect.

I was self-controlled.

I was not a malicious talker.

I was faithful in all things.

Test: Ask each person to take the "Pop Test" under her chair.

Reports

1. Last week we discussed eight ways a deacon wife could make a difference this week. Would someone like to share which one you worked on this week and the results of your effort?

2. We've challenged everyone to make one homebound, nursing home, or sick visit during these six weeks. If you did yours this week, we'd love to hear one testimony about how it went (testimony; planned or not).

Lecture: Prepare a ten-minute lecture about what the Bible says about encouragement and how that applies to deacon wives at your church. Challenge each deacon wife to encourage others. Lead a conversation about encouraging new Christians, female visitors, and children. Talk about ways to encourage your pastor.

Share: Guide women to turn their chairs so they can discuss the following with their prayer partner.

1. Turn to your prayer partner and give her a sincere compliment. Encouragement feels good, doesn't it?

2. Tell your prayer partner one good thing about your deacon husband and his ministry in our church.

3. Tell your prayer partner one new or renewed commitment you made this week about encouragement (i.e., I plan to listen during church to encourage my pastor).

Homework (distribute early): Distribute homework assignment sheets before church staff wives arrive. Review assignments. Show ladies their photos on the wall in groups of two and let them know that is their new prayer partner for the next two weeks. As women get their photos, they should exchange them with their prayer partners, who may want to put photos on their refrigerator as a reminder to pray.

Homework Assignment for Session 3

_____ Read these Scriptures slowly: 1 Corinthians 7:3–5, Song of Songs 7:1–9.

_____ Do one thing to encourage your pastor's wife this week. (See pages 55–56 in book.)

_____ Review 1 Timothy 3:11. (There will be a test.)

_____ Pray for your new prayer partner. Sometime during the next two weeks, try to meet her for lunch or coffee or make a ministry visit together.

_____ Read chapter 3 in your *Deacon Wives* book.

_____ Bring a family snapshot next week.

Pastor's Wife: When the pastor's wife (and staff wives, if applicable) arrives, pose quickly for a group photo with her standing in the center of the group.

Ask the pastor's wife to sit in the chair at the center of the V and additional staff wives and female staff to sit by her. Read Proverbs 25:11 (apple verse), then allow each deacon wife to say a sentence of encouragement to the pastor's or ministers' wives, and present her an apple. If your staff is large, divide deacon wives between staff wives for this activity.

Closing Prayer: Deacon officers' wives lead a closing prayer of commitment to encourage others.

Session 3: Home and Family

Preparation

1. Invite the pastor to come by to offer your opening prayer if he is available.
2. Prepare a framed copy of the photo of deacon wives with pastor's wife as a gift for the pastor. If you have additional staff wives, make a copy for each of them.
3. Write "open book test" from chapter 3 on whiteboard, leaving blanks.
4. Make copies of "Ways I've Used My Home," "Spiritual Gifts Survey," and "My Ministry in My Church."
5. Finalize photo page or directory for deacons' wives for distribution.
6. Optional: Place a small round fishbowl with one fish inside on a table in the center of the circle. The person with a ☺ on the back of her name tag gets to take the fish home afterward.

Setup: Put chairs in a large circle. If your group is larger than ten, make circles of ten or less. Leave up last week's sign asking women to sit by prayer partner.

Arrival: As ladies arrive, present them your photo page or directory of deacon wives.

Opening: After pastor offers the opening prayer, present him with a framed photo of his wife with the deacon wives before he leaves.

Introductory Activity: Photo Op: Ask the deacon wife with the ❤ on the back of her name tag to show her family photo to the group and introduce each family member in the photo. Set a timer for five minutes and ask ladies to walk around and show their family photo to other deacon wives.

Report: Did anyone personally welcome a newcomer at church last Sunday? Would one of you like to share what you did to welcome them? Do you remember her name?

Complete the open book test on the whiteboard as a group.

Two-Word Discussions: Ask the following questions, one at a time; then go counterclockwise around the circle for each person to answer with only two words.

1. Say your first and last name. (Skip this if everyone already knows names.)
2. Say two words that describe your church.
3. What color is your sofa?
4. What's your most famous dish you prepare. (Even red Jell-O is fine!)
5. If my children described our family in two words, they would say _____.

Lecture: Prepare a brief Bible study and challenge about the importance of family and the privilege of using our homes for Christ. Discuss the fishbowl and the importance of setting a good example. (Inform the person with the ☺ on the back of her name tag that she wins the fish to take home!) Talk about using our homes for ministry and distribute "Ways I've Used My Home to Minister in the Past Year" form. Allow women to brainstorm ideas for using homes to enhance church ministry.

Prayer: Ask that each older woman pair with a younger woman for the closing prayer and pray for her family.

Prayer Partners: Announce that women will keep the same prayer partner for an additional week. Keep on praying!

Homework Assignment for Session 4

_____ Consider one new way you can use your home to serve God.

_____ Consider one improvement you can implement to improve your family.

_____ Do the "silent witness" exercise on page 76 of this book.

_____ Pray for your prayer partner. Meet for coffee if possible.

_____ Review 1 Timothy 3:11.

_____ Read chapter 4 in your *Deacon Wives* book.

Session 4: The D Word

Preparation: Make copies of "Mid-term Quiz" (page 81), printed practice prayer requests, homework assignment, My Ministry form, and Spiritual Gifts survey.

Copy "Some Words from the Word about Words" and cut each Scripture into individual strips.

Prepare birthday month signs for group division. Play recorded music.

Room Setup: Put chairs in circles of three or four. In the center of each circle, lay a poster sign to divide ladies by birth month. (For example, a group of seven deacon wives could have a January-June circle and a July-December group. A larger group of wives could have a circle for each month.)

Arrival: As ladies arrive, recorded music is playing. Give each woman a pencil, a midterm exam, and a few of the Scriptures about gossip. Ask them to please sit in the circle for their birth month and complete their midterm exam quietly.

Opening: The deacon chairman's wife leads an opening prayer a couple of minutes after class start time and welcomes deacon wives.

New Prayer Partners: Ask women to select a woman in their birthday-month group to be their prayer partner this week. They can exchange names and phone numbers at this time. Encourage them to meet for coffee or a ministry visit, or meet together before or after church for a few minutes.

Quiet Game: As you read the following phrases, each woman will communicate her answer to her group, but she cannot use her voice. Total silence!

1. How many years have you been married?
2. What's your favorite time of day?
3. How long have you been a Christian?
4. How do you look when you wake up in the morning?
5. Communicate this phrase nonverbally: "I don't approve!"

Prayer Request Rehearsal: This exercise will demonstrate how to use discretion in making prayer requests in a public church setting. Each person in the group receives one of the printed prayer requests below. After reading it, they determine appropriate words to request prayer for this person. This exercise may help them to use discretion in giving private details. (No report back necessary.)

Janice Davenport has been informed that she has cancer. They have located it in her esophagus in a node the size of a lemon. She and her husband Joe already had marital problems, and this may put their marriage over the edge. Her youngest daughter is the head cheerleader at our high school, and her son has had recent problems with SAT scores. She will begin aggressive chemo as soon as her vital signs average a normal range. (Currently her blood pressure is at 250.)

Mandy Jordash, a single mother with a donated sperm implant pregnancy, gave birth today to a son, Jamie Leslie, at Hudson General Hospital. The baby weighed thirteen pounds, two ounces (largest baby born in our church this year), and there was a small problem with torn cartilage. Baby and mother are doing fine now. Mandy helps in our church's youth Sunday school.

Betty Ingram, a church member, invited you for coffee last week so she could ask your opinion about some financial and personal decisions. Specifically, she is having some problems with overspending and with marital fidelity. Her dog's name is Foofoo.

Your husband mentioned a potential problem that was discussed at last week's deacons meeting. The pastor and stewardship committee are considering rearranging the missions giving expenditures.

In a humorous way you can help women realize that many details above should not be voiced in a group, and some of the requests should not be spoken at all!

Lecture: Prepare a brief Bible lesson and challenge about gossip and discretion as it applies to deacon wives. At the end ask women to take their Bibles and Scripture reading assignments and stand in a large circle around the room.

Circle Readings: Women randomly read their assigned Scriptures aloud. Each Scripture addresses gossip. It will take about ten minutes, but it will demonstrate the seriousness of using discretion in our speech. Conclude with a challenge to be women of discretion and never to gossip.

Write these Scriptures individually on a piece of paper and divide them among deacon wives for reading.

Some Words from the Word about Words
"A gossip goes around revealing a secret, but the trustworthy keeps a confidence" (Prov. 11:13).
"A contrary man spreads conflict, and a gossip separates friends" (Prov. 16:28).
"The one who reveals secrets is a constant gossip; avoid someone with a big mouth" (Prov. 20:19).
"Without wood, fire goes out; without a gossip, conflict dies down" (Prov. 26:20).
"Should he argue with useless talk or with words that serve no good purpose?" (Job 15:3).
"All of you have seen this for yourselves, why do you keep up this empty talk?" (Job 27:12).
"Those who sit at the city gate talk about me, and drunkards make up songs about me" (Ps. 69:12).
"Don't let your mouth speak dishonestly, and don't let your lips talk deviously" (Prov. 4:24).
"There is profit in all hard work, but endless talk leads only to poverty" (Prov. 14:23).
"A wicked person listens to malicious talk; a liar pays attention to a destructive tongue" (Prov. 17:4).

"Don't criticize one another" (James 4:11).
"They are filled with all unrighteousness, evil, greed, and wickedness. They are full of envy, murder, disputes, deceit, and malice. They are gossips" (Rom. 1:29).
"But now you must also put away all the following: anger, wrath, malice, slander, and filthy language from your mouth" (Col. 3:8).
"You must not go about spreading slander among your people; you must not jeopardize your neighbor's life; I am the LORD" (Lev. 19:16).
"The one who conceals hatred has lying lips, and whoever spreads slander is a fool" (Prov. 10:18).
"Don't slander a servant to his master, or he will curse you, and you will become guilty" (Prov. 30:10).
"All bitterness, anger and wrath, insult and slander must be removed from you, along with all wickedness" (Eph. 4:31).
"To slander no one, to avoid fighting, and to be kind, always showing gentleness to all people" (Titus 3:2).
"So rid yourselves of all wickedness, all deceit, hypocrisy, envy, and all slander" (1 Pet. 2:1).
"The LORD detests the plans of an evil man, but pleasant words are pure" (Prov. 15:26).
"Cursing, deceit, and violence fill his mouth; trouble and malice are under his tongue" (Ps. 10:7).
"You have tested my heart; You have visited by night; You have tried me and found nothing evil; I have determined that my mouth will not sin" (Ps. 17:3).
"The words of his mouth are malicious and deceptive; he has stopped acting wisely and doing good" (Ps. 36:3).

"The mouth of the righteous utters wisdom; his tongue speaks what is just" (Ps. 37:30).

"I said, 'I will guard my ways so that I may not sin with my tongue; I will guard my mouth with a muzzle as long as the wicked are in my presence'" (Ps. 39:1).

"You unleash your mouth for evil and harness your tongue for deceit" (Ps. 50:19).

"LORD, set up a guard for my mouth; keep watch at the door of my lips" (Ps. 141:3).

"You have been trapped by the words of your lips—ensnared by the words of your mouth" (Prov. 6:2).

"The wise store up knowledge, but the mouth of the fool hastens destruction" (Prov. 10:14).

"The mouth of the righteous produces wisdom, but a perverse tongue will be cut out" (Prov. 10:31).

"The lips of the righteous know what is appropriate, but the mouth of the wicked, only what is perverse" (Prov. 10:32).

"The one who guards his mouth protects his life; the one who opens his lips invites his own ruin" (Prov. 13:3).

"The proud speech of a fool brings a rod of discipline, but the lips of the wise protect them" (Prov. 14:3).

"The tongue of the wise makes knowledge attractive, but the mouth of fools blurts out foolishness" (Prov. 15:2).

"A discerning mind seeks knowledge, but the mouth of fools feeds on foolishness" (Prov. 15:14).

"The mind of the righteous person thinks before answering, but the mouth of the wicked blurts out evil things" (Prov. 15:28).

"A fool's lips lead to strife, and his mouth provokes a beating" (Prov. 18:6).

"A fool's mouth is his devastation, and his lips are a trap for his life" (Prov. 18:7).

"A worthless witness mocks justice, and a wicked mouth swallows iniquity" (Prov. 19:28).

"The one who guards his mouth and tongue keeps himself out of trouble" (Prov. 21:23).

"A lying tongue hates those it crushes, and a flattering mouth causes ruin" (Prov. 26:28).

"The words from the mouth of a wise man are gracious, but the lips of a fool consume him" (Eccl. 10:12).

"Brood of vipers! How can you speak good things when you are evil? For the mouth speaks from the overflow of the heart" (Matt. 12:34).

"A good man produces good out of the good storeroom of his heart. An evil man produces evil out of the evil storeroom, for his mouth speaks from the overflow of the heart" (Luke 6:45).

"No rotten talk should come from your mouth, but only what is good for the building up of someone in need, in order to give grace to those who hear" (Eph. 4:29).

"Out of the same mouth come blessing and cursing. My brothers, these things should not be this way" (James 3:10).

"Wives, too, must be worthy of respect, not slanderers, self-controlled, faithful in everything" (1 Tim. 3:11).

(Read this Scripture last.) "May the words of my mouth and the meditation of my heart be acceptable to You, LORD, my rock and my Redeemer" (Ps. 19:14).

Wrap-up: Distribute assignment sheets and lead a prayer asking God to convict deacon wives of the importance of discretion.

Homework Assignment for Session 5

_____ Complete "My Ministry" form, attached.

_____ Complete Spiritual Gifts Survey, attached.

_____ Pray with your prayer partner. Try to meet together sometime this week for fellowship or a ministry visit.

_____ Read chapter 5 in your *Deacon Wives* book.

Session 5: Ministry Tips

Preparation
- Make copies of "ring-ring" activity.
- Prepare seven posters or tear sheets with these seven headings:
  - ! My spiritual gift is:
  - ! Ideas/comments for ministering to sick
  - ! Ideas/comments about ministering during bereavement
  - ! Ideas/comments about ministering at nursing homes
  - ! Ideas/comments about ministering to homebound
  - ! Ideas/comments about ministering to lonely
  - ! Ideas/comments about ministering in crisis
- Provide a black marker for each deacon wife.
- Write on whiteboard: Questions for prayer partner discussion, below.
- Prepare a current listing of homebound church members and those in local nursing homes.

Room Setup: Chairs are placed in curved rows with lecturer at the front.

Put the whiteboard to the side of the room near the entrance.

Hang seven posters or tear sheets (above) on walls around the room.

Arrival: As women arrive, give each person a marker, and ask women to write something on each of six posters around the room before they are seated.

Lecture: Prepare a brief lecture about the joy of ministering to others in Christ's name. Give specific examples of ways deacon wives in your church have made a difference. Use the posters to demonstrate how God has gifted each woman differently. Talk about specific ways deacon wives can help at your church.

At the end of your lecture, arrange for someone to dial your cell phone so it rings while you're talking. Answer it and say: "Oh ladies, it's for you! There's a crisis in the church. Let's see how you'll handle it. Please divide into groups of three or four, move your chairs together, and I'll bring you your phone message." Quickly distribute these messages, asking groups to make a sample plan for immediate ministry action.

"Ring-Ring" Exercise: Each small group receives one message and discusses how they might react.

1. "Ring. Ring." You receive a phone call that a tornado just went through the middle of your town. You don't know details yet, but you know it's serious.
2. "Ring. Ring." A church member calls to tell you his next-door neighbor had a gas explosion in his home while he was at work, just half an hour ago. It's a total loss.
3. "Ring. Ring." The pastor just called. Lightning struck your church building, and water is pouring in.
4. "Ring. Ring." A church member has died.

Prayer Partners: Explain that the ring-ring exercise was planned to help them to think ahead about how God can use them in crisis. (No report-back on this assignment.) Ask women to move into groups of two, pairing with someone new as a prayer partner. Invite prayer partners to discuss the four questions written on the whiteboard:

1. What do you feel is your spiritual gift (from spiritual gifts homework page)?

2. Tell about areas of ministry in the church where you feel God is using you or could use you. (Note: In the next class you will share about your prayer partner's favorite ministry.)
3. Can you and I make a ministry visit this week together?
4. Pray aloud for your prayer partner to have wisdom in serving God.

Dismissal: Distribute homebound list and homework assignment and lead in a dismissal prayer.

Homework Assignment for Session 6

_____ Ministry visit: If possible, make a ministry visit with your prayer partner this week. It can be an outreach visit, sick visit, benevolence, bereavement, homebound, crisis, etc. We'll report on these visits next week.

_____ Review 1 Timothy 3:11 for "final exam."

_____ Read chapter 6 in your _Deacon Wives_ book.

Session 6: Worth the Effort

Preparation

1. Invite the pastor to stop by for the first few minutes of class to have refreshments and visit informally with deacon wives.
2. Invite the pastor's wife and ministry staff wives to attend the entire closing session if they are available. Let them know you would like deacon wives to hear their ideas and dreams of ways deacon wives could assist that staff wife and the church in ministry.
3. Prepare a printed list of deacon wives' names for the pastor's wife. Ask if she would give a brief word of closing and encouragement to deacon wives and present each of them with a flower and photo.
4. Make copies of final exam.
5. Print a group photo (from Session 1) for each deacon wife. If budget allows, put them in small frames.
6. Make a centerpiece for the reception, using fresh long-stemmed flowers that have individual watering tips. They will be presented individually during a closing ceremony.
7. Purchase an inexpensive tea towel or hand towel for each deacon wife.
8. Plan refreshments and taped music during snacks.

Room Setup: Chairs are set in multiple half circles for a reception-style fellowship. A serving table is set with drinks, snacks, pretty napkins, and flowers.

Write the question from "In Summary" exercise on the white-board or a poster.

Arrival: As ladies arrive, invite them to have drinks and snacks and fellowship together for a few minutes.

Opening: Introduce the pastor and thank him for joining the group for snacks. Ask him to lead the group in prayer before he leaves. Introduce pastoral staff wives and welcome them. Invite them to participate in class.

Just Numbers: Read each phrase below, and ask each woman quickly to say her response as a number. (No discussion; just say the number!)

My age when I accepted Christ as my Savior

Number of newcomers I welcomed at church last Sunday

Number of children, grandchildren, and great-grandchildren I have (total)

Number of pastors I've had during my lifetime

Number of deacon wives I've grown to love during these past six weeks

Reports:

1. Ask each deacon wife to introduce her prayer partner from last week and briefly tell about her prayer partner's favorite ministry in the church. (Just one.) If your group is large, this activity may be done in smaller groups.

2. If any prayer partners made a ministry visit together during the week, ask for one or two brief reports.

Ministry Needs in Our Church: If yours is a single-staff-member church, all women gather their chairs around the pastor's wife for a few minutes of Q&A. The purpose of this time is to ask for her ideas for ways deacon wives can help with needs in the church.

If you have multiple staff members, each of them sits in a different area of the room, and deacon wives divide themselves (fairly evenly) among the staff wives. Deacon wives may ask questions related to their expertise and interests. Encourage them to share specific ways they see deacon wives could help or enhance ministry in the church.

After about ten minutes of discussion, invite the oldest deacon wife in each group to voice a prayer for that ministry wife.

In Summary: The deacon chairman's wife points women to the summary question on the whiteboard and asks a couple of volunteers to respond.

> How has this study encouraged you as a deacon wife?

She issues a final challenge to deacon wives to be servants in the church and presents a small towel to each woman in the Scripture from Galations 5:13 to challenge deacon wives to joyfully serve others in our church. She invites the pastor's wife to share a closing word. Leave ten minutes for the closing ceremony with pastor's wife.

Closing Ceremony: In a brief closing ceremony, the pastor's wife can share a personal word of encouragement to deacon wives. She then calls the name of each deacon wife, using a printed list, and presents her with a flower from the vase and a group photo. *Alternate:* the church may want to prepare personalized certificates. She leads the group in a closing prayer.

Take-Home Test: As deacon wives exit, give them a copy of the take-home final exam.

If deacons and deacon wives have had simultaneous training, consider planning a fellowship together.